A
SHORT HISTORY GUIDE
TO
PORT ARTHUR
1830-77

By

Alex Graeme-Evans

- view of Champ Street past Administrative office leading to the Commandant's house -
(COURTESY TASMANIAN MUSEUM AND ART GALLERY)

PREFACE

This is a personalised short history of the Port Arthur Penal Settlement (1830-77), located on the Tasman Peninsula south of Hobart. It is designed to heighten the appreciation of the general visitor, and to serve as an interesting resource aid for school teachers planning to take their classes on excursion. While visiting Port Arthur we recommend that the Port Arthur Historic Site Management Authority's location map brochure, is read in conjunction with this publication.

If upon reading the history, you come away with an underlying appreciation not only of the intrinsic importance of the Port Arthur Settlement in terms of Australian pioneering history, but also that it serves as a monument to the existence here at an earlier era, of one of the most significant British Imperial prisons ever constructed outside the British Isles, then the major objectives of this short history will have been achieved.

Please now proceed to wander around the historic site either with a Guide or on your own with the PAHS location brochure and this book to assist you.

In putting this short history together we would like to thank the Port Arthur Historic Site Management Authority, the Tasmanian Museum and Art Gallery, the Tasmania Media Centre Department of Education and the Arts, the Archives Office of Tasmania (and the owners of the other art material) for their support with respect to the republication of various sketches, lithographs and photographs that have provided greater depth to the text. Finally we would like to thank Richard Bracey of Regal Press Tasmania in ensuring that this Second Edition (the First was sold out within three months of the launch), has met with a smooth passage so that the books are back once more on the retailers' book-shelves.

Alex Graeme-Evans

- a view of Port Arthur in the 1870s from Scorpion Hill with the church in the foreground -
(COURTESY ARCHIVES OFFICE OF TASMANIA)

Dedication: *to those who as victims of social pressures in England in the early nineteenth century, suffered greatly under the British Transportation Penal System, and who after release never recovered from the experience.*

About the Authors:

Michael Ross is a Guide at the Port Arthur Historic Site and lives at Koonya with his wife Sue and their four children Leigh, Alex, Kieran and Sean. Unlike the convicts that are the subject of this short history of Port Arthur, Michael chose freely to emigrate to the Tasman Peninsula to enjoy the quality of life Tasmania has to offer there.

Alex Graeme-Evans JP is a Tasmanian Historian and former Senior Executive Officer of the Tasmanian National Parks and Wildlife Service. He lives at Woodbridge in the D'Entrecasteaux Channel with his wife Margo and their three children Joshua, Andrew and Sarah. Alex's resolve to research and write in this area was initiated many years ago when he studied under one of Australia's foremost Legal Historians, Professor A.C. Castles at Adelaide University.

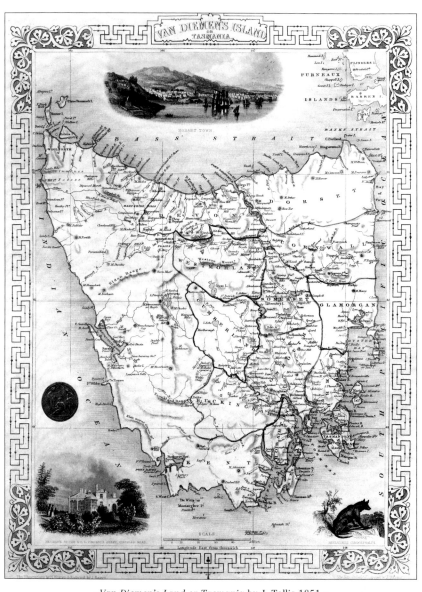

- Van Diemen's Land or Tasmania by J. Tallis 1851 -
(Tasmaniana Collection State Library of Tasmania)

- Convict Ships - Port of Hobart -
(COURTESY PORT ARTHUR COLLECTION)

CONTENTS
Port Arthur - The Imperial Prison

Introduction
Chapter One: Transportation - *a fate worse than death* .... pages 3-9
Chapter Two: The Laying of Foundations 1830-33... pages 10-15
Chapter Three: Consolidation 1834-44 .... pages 16-32
Chapter Four: Holding the Line 1844-49 .... pages 33-36
Chapter Five: A Period of Irreversible Change 1849-53 .... pages 37-41
Chapter Six: A Time of Shame 1853-56 .... pages 42-53
Chapter Seven: End of an Era 1856-77.. pages 54-58

Appendices: Suggested Further Reading
Centrefold: *Statistical Minutes* of the Boys Establishment Point Puer - Half Year
ending 30/6/1837.

Painting Above: Not generally appreciated, it is a tribute to the British Authorities that great care was taken as to the seaworthiness of the ships and the quality of the crews engaged to convey convicts to the Antipodes. Of the 160,663 convicts transported to Australia in those comparatively small ships, less than 550 were lost at sea due to shipwreck or misadventure. Slightly in excess of 67,000 of these convicts were sent direct to Van Diemen's Land (V.D.L.).

INTRODUCTION

Without visual aids such as photographs, few visitors would be aware or could conceive (in viewing what remains today), of the diversity of trades that were practised here at Port Arthur in the early 1840s. For instance, at Point Puer just across the bay from the main settlement, some 800 boy convicts were housed in their own dormitories and attended school until apprenticed in a trade of their choice at the age of 12/13 years.

In this regard Port Arthur for a time, led the English speaking world in the way it treated delinquent boys. Indeed, the success of the programme at Port Arthur (of juveniles being kept separate and treated differently from the adult prisoners) in part caused its own demise, for it set a precedent which the Prison Authorities back in England, would ultimately follow. While the discipline then was harsh in today's terms, it is clear the boy convicts at Port Arthur were better cared for and received better education in a regularised fashion (again another first), than ever they would have received had they continued their lives in the disease-ridden alleys of the large English industrial towns of that era.

So that you can more fully appreciate the 'feel' of those times as you tour the historic site, we have chosen to commence the story of Port Arthur with the background details as to How and Why transportation became a reality in pre-industrial, and industrial Great Britain. We then follow with the relationship of Australia to such a penal system, and how in turn Tasmania (then named Van Diemen's Land), and Port Arthur fitted into this larger picture.

The picture is not a pretty one; of the British Government under the auspices of its judicial system, transporting people in very hazardous circumstances in small ships across the globe from their native homes to a remote foreign land; a distant place from which comparatively few returned.

The balance of the short history then deals with the various phases in the life of Port Arthur from its early beginnings as a penal settlement, to that of an important Imperial prison of the British government. In its way the rise into prominence and then fading into disuse of the Port Arthur prison, mirrors in reverse form, the development of the state of Tasmania, on its own tortuous path towards colonial self-government.

CHAPTER ONE

Transportation - a fate worse than death

Human nature has not changed over the past centuries. The practice of transportation was not by any means a new concept when Port Arthur, located on the Tasman Peninsula in southern Van Diemen's Land (Tasmania), was first decided on as an appropriate site for a penal colony. Indeed it was mere chance. An urgent need had arisen in the late 1820s, for a good man-handling saw-log timbered site, to replace the earlier station at Birchs Bay in the D'Entrecasteaux Channel, south of Hobart. The governor at that time was Governor Arthur, who in the end chose the Tasman Peninsula site (which is named after him) since it is from a sailing ship's perspective, relatively close to Hobart. The other less favourable option at that time under active consideration, had been the wilds of King Island, to the distant north. However, before considering in detail the history of the settlement of this unique Imperial prison, it is meaningful for us to consider first, how *'convictism'* began.

Pressures of Social Circumstance

When Queen Elizabeth I ascended to the throne in 1558, times in England were very uncertain. However, under her skilled rule that nation's mercantile powers were able to blossom, subsequent to the defeat of the *'Spanish Armada'* (prior to which the English Admiral Drake calmly played bowls on land whilst waiting for the aggressor's invasion fleet to arrive!). Such powers were consolidated further after the successful outcome for England of the subsequent series of naval battles against the Dutch maritime fleets. From that period on, the British navy became very much the master of the ocean trade routes to the New World and elsewhere.

A side benefit of such mercantile power was that successive British Governments were able (as a form of social expediency), to *transport* unwanted persons away from their 'fair realm', to places distant and remote.

First Major Experiment

The first major experiment of using *transportation* as a means of dealing with persons considered to be 'undesirable' (be they criminals or religious heretics), occurred in the reign of James I in 1607. A new frontier establishment was set up (named after the King) at Jamestown, on the Chesapeake River in the American state of Virginia. At that time convicts were transported to Jamestown and then rather like an Arabian bazaar of more recent times, auctioned off to the highest bidders to serve as slaves (euphemistically referred to as being 'indentured labourers') for the period of their sentence. Most had sentences in the order of 10 years duration, with the most common crime being petty theft.

Concept of Transportation Regularised in 1718

In 1718 the English House of Commons in London passed the **Transportation Act.** This Act of the British Houses of Parliament regularised the concept of transportation, so that it might serve as a central remedy available to the courts, when dealing with the ever increasing crime-wave experienced as a result of the over-crowding of the large country towns and cities in England.

Britain at this time was at the forefront of the Industrial Revolution, which in turn was forcing peasants off the land away from their agrarian occupations. Now penniless, starving, and without a trade, such families were converging in ever increasing numbers into the dingy unhygienic streets of the major cities to look for work and sustenance for their families.

Law and order became a major issue in society, and one way of avoiding the rigours of Capital punishment (e.g. putting someone to death by means of hanging), was to commute the sentence by *an act of mercy* (in cases where the conviction related to comparatively minor breaches such as petty theft) to that of banishment - *transportation*.

While the concept of transportation, as debated in the hallowed halls of Parliament, was considered to be a humanistic way of dealing with the poor and destitute (steering 'the accused' away from a life of crime), it was for the victims of these court rulings, a far different perception. Transportation to them, was seen as *'a fate worse than death'*.

To the court-ruled *'undesirables',* drawn principally from the starving and unemployed segments of the lower working classes in England, the sentence of transportation was seen as a brutal form of punishment. It took them not only from their familiar surroundings and loved ones but also, without their consent, pitched them into the unknown, with comparatively few ever returning to the English, Scottish, Welsh or Irish County of their birth.

American States Declaration of Independence - 1776

Until 1776 America was still the major destination for those exiled from Great Britain under the Transportation system. During this period some 60,000 convicts were transported across the Atlantic to American states such as Maryland, Virginia, South Carolina, and Georgia. In 1776 the watershed **Declaration of Independence** from Great Britain by the American states occurred, and a new remote destination to which convicted felons could be sent, had to be found. Another ten years of trial and error (1) were now to pass, until Australia was settled on as the new *'off-shore prison'* for British felons.

Use of Hulks as an Interim Measure

As an interim measure 'hulks' (disused and out-of-service naval ships) moored off the coast at Plymouth, Portsmouth, and Southampton and estuaries of rivers such as the Thames, were used to accommodate the ever increasing wave of persons convicted of petty crime. All were victims of the increased pace of the New Industrial Age which was now taking hold in Great Britain. In the process it was destroying piecemeal the agrarian social infrastructure, which previously had been the mainstay of British society.

*- etching by Edward Cooke 1828 of the **HMS Discovery** at Deptford -*
(COURTESY PORT ARTHUR COLLECTION)

This perceived increased level of crime by the socially disadvantaged, the starving and the unemployed, and the ever increasing evidence of their resulting plight in the overcrowded hulks, now induced a sense of panic amongst the wealthy and prosperous industrialised middle-classes in the major urban areas of Britain.

Sanitation was non existent in the hulks and there was a constant threat of the spread of disease to the general public through the agency of escapees. This visual festering symbol of human misery could not be politically ignored. By the early 1780s, talk started to abound in influential circles: that a new destination for convicted felons should be found, now that the North American states had closed their doors on such forced migration.

The Influence of Joseph Banks

So it was in 1786 (with the persuasive arguments of Joseph Banks who had first-hand experience of conditions in Australia from the time he had served as botanist to James Cook in his famous voyage on the good ship ***HMS Endeavour***), that the decision was made to provision an expedition to claim Australia for King George III of Great Britain. In audiences with King George of England, Joseph Banks was convincing in his arguments as to the suitability of Australia to perform such a role. In so doing, he overcame the alternative options presented by his close friend Jeremy Bentham, one of the leading prison reformers in Great Britain at that time. Joseph Banks can be truly seen therefore, as not only a great botanist but also the major catalyst for the colonisation of Australia by a foreign European power in the late eighteenth century.

Departure of the First Fleet - 1787

The group of ships which subsequently became known as 'The First Fleet', left Portsmouth on the 13th May 1787, under the command of Governor Arthur Phillip. The aim of the mission was to open up a British gateway to the Pacific, locate and occupy a stop-off point for the trade routes to China, and to locate a suitable dumping ground for *the felons of England*.

After many trials and tribulations the fleet finally arrived at Botany Bay in late January 1788, and the British flag was formally raised to denote possession of the land at the site now known as Port Jackson, on the 26th of that month. There were eleven ships in the Fleet and they were like *corks on the ocean* for, from 'stem to stern', their combined length would be less than that of a modern oil tanker. Apart from 1482 people (of which 778 were convicted felons (2)), there was amongst the livestock only 1 bullock, 3 cows and 44 sheep, which survived the journey.

From all accounts, due to haste, the expedition had been inadequately organised and extreme privation was to follow. (3) Battling the elements in New South Wales was to keep the small Sydney Town colony fully occupied for many years. However in 1803, a young and inexperienced Lieutenant John Bowen was despatched in the *Lady Nelson*, to set up a permanent British settlement in southern Van Diemen's Land - the large island located to the south of the continent of Australia. It had first been discovered by the Dutch explorer Abel Tasman some 161 years earlier in 1642.

Occupation of Van Diemen's Land by British Forces - 1803

The purpose of this mission (as conceived by the British Colonial authorities), was to thwart presumed French Government designs to take over control of the island. The Nationalistic 'scramble for foreign lands', by dominant European countries, was now at the start of the nineteenth century, in full flight. With their inherent belief in the superiority of their cultures and technology, European explorers and statesmen considered the *'hunter-gatherer'* state of aboriginals living on the mainland and on this island at that time to be that of the status of savages, not of a *civilised society*. Hence, the land was legally considered to be *'terra nullus'* (vacant land). (4)

Under such a doctrine of International law, Lieutenant Bowen declared Van Diemen's Land for King George of Great Britain by a simple symbolic act of planting a flag, military gun-fire salutes (and the reading of a carefully-worded document). From then on, it was deemed that British law had now extended to this large most southern island of the Antipodes.

The Creation of Hobart Town

In February 1804 Lieutenant Governor David Collins, a far more experienced military commander arrived and found the site of Risdon Cove on the eastern shore of the River Derwent, as settled on by Lieutenant Bowen, to be unsatisfactory. Collins now relocated the site of this first major European settlement in V.D.L. across the river to the western shore, to the place now known as Sullivans Cove. It is on this second site that the 'Hobart Town', with which we are familiar today, both prospered and grew.

Prisons within Prisons

Concerns as to the ease of escape to the hinterlands of New South Wales from Sydney Town, combined with a clear understanding that there were emerging two types of convicts (those that were amenable to reform and those that were not), seeded the idea in the minds of the colonial establishment in Australia, that the setting up of a secondary type of penal settlement was now timely.

Further, it was proposed, that the secondary settlement for the 'hard cases', should be more remote and located in inhospitable terrain; so that the 'incorrigibles' might not dampen the 'social air' and well-being of the residents of Sydney Town.

In practice, such a sifting of the convicts had already been under way for several years. Under Governor Collins' stewardship, followed by successive Governors, the Vandemonian settlement to the south of the Australian continent had continued to grow slowly, and by 1817 there was a population of some 5,000 Europeans. Approximately half were under sentence as convicts. Most of the latter had been transported from the mainland as *second offenders'*.

Pressures of a Continental Peace

Concurrent with the local policy that had emerged to shift the hard case 'second offenders' to Van Diemen's Land, was the successful conclusion in far-off Europe of the Continental war with France. A conservative government was in power in England, and the colonies of Australia then established were now seen as a panacea for the chronic overcrowding of the English cities. Crime rates had continued to climb with not only the unemployed, but also demobbed soldiers contributing to the problems of a nation seeking to recover from a long and costly war.

- sketch by emigrant artist Private Edward Murphy -
(COURTESY PORT ARTHUR COLLECTION)

Shift in Emphasis towards Van Diemen's Land (Tasmania)

Active emigration was now encouraged out of England, be it as freemen or alternatively under sentence. A new large tidal-swell of convicts began to arrive in Australia. For the first time convicts were being sent direct to Van Diemen's Land

It was not a happy society for the freemen, who had began to land in increasing numbers in Hobart Town. Upon arrival they found that alongside newly landed convicts from the 'mother country', they also encountered hard-case second offenders from the mainland. Harsh discipline had to be imposed to keep order by the authorities, and after years of curfews and flagrant thefts, pressure was increasingly applied on local government administrators to remove from the more commercial and populous areas of the island, the *'incorrigibles'*. (5)

Settlements at Macquarie and Maria Islands

Macquarie Harbour followed by Maria Island were the first tentative steps in this direction, but proved unsuccessful for a number of reasons. (6) The next consideration was King Island in the Bass Strait. However here politics intervened. The new governor for V.D.L. Governor George Arthur, did not wish to be beholden to Directors of the Van Diemen's Land Company for the securing of likely escapees. It is for this reason we return once more to the cutting of timber, and the inadequacy of the timber groves at Birchs Bay in the Channel area, of Southern Tasmania.

- Governor George Arthur -

Tasman Peninsula

East Bay Neck

Forestier's Peninsula

Slopen Island

Coal Mines

Norfolk Bay

Mt Wilson
Saltwater River

Woody Island

Eaglehawk Neck

Price's Bay

Norfolk Bay Station

Mt Communication

Cascades

Parson's Bay

Signal Hill

Tasman's Peninsula

Wedge Bay

N
W — E
S

Stewart's Bay

PORT ARTHUR
Pt Puer
Mt Arthur

Mt Fortesque

Arthur's Peak

KEY
Signal stations
Old tramway

Cape Raoul

Tasman's Island

A Fateful Surveyor's Report

As fate would have it, surveyors in the late 1820s had reported to the colonial administration, that they had found a new potential timber station on the Tasman Peninsula: *'a deep and safe harbour, with stands of timber on all sides coming down to the water's edge'*. The Surveyors also, *'with profound respect'*, sought permission of the Governor to name the convenient harbour in his honour - **Port Arthur**.

This timely report swayed the pendulum of chance. The Deputy Surveyor-General Thomas Scott, provided a second opinion strongly in favour in December 1828: that it was in the very centre of fine timber, extending in a semi-circle - 'about 7 miles, by from 1 to 2 in width'.

Orders were finally issued to set up a settlement at Port Arthur on the 7th September 1830, with the operations at Birchs Bay closing down and the working and hut framing materials there transferred to Port Arthur. Public knowledge of the new venture was broadcast several days later, highlighting the wealth-generating aspects of the operation for which the author of one report concluded - *'the Government is entitled to much praise for undertaking it'*, and that the settlement would serve as a *'half-way house'* for convicts: not as remote or severe as Macquarie Harbour, but not as close as the Hobart Penitentiary!

And so it was in late September 1830, that Captain Assistant-Surgeon John Russell of the 63rd Regiment of Foot, supervised the disembarking of his men (and hand-selected convicts from Macquarie Harbour), onto the shore of the New Settlement at Port Arthur. A new era in Australian convictism had begun.

Footnotes :
1. Wilfred Oldham's publication entitled *'Britain's Convicts to the Colonies'* Library of Australia 1990, covers well this period. There was first a limited re-opening of the traffic to the American states 1783-85, and then an experiment in West Africa at an island called Le Maine some 450 miles up the Gambia River in 1785-86. However this experiment ended in failure due to a high incidence of sickness at the settlement (Yellow fever).
2. There has been much debate over the years by historians as to exactly how many convicts came ashore as part of the First Fleet contingent. Much of it has been a matter of interpretation. With the stigma of having 'convict roots' no longer being regarded as a family skeleton, the expanded figure as recently quoted by Stephen Nicholas in *'Convict Worker'*, Cambridge University Press Sydney 1988, is accepted as being the most accurate.
3. The experiences and privations suffered by members of the First Fleet and the growth of Sydney Town in the course of those fifteen years, falls outside the province of this history. However while not exhaustive, the following two books provide two different perspectives on this subject and can be therefore classed as additional reading: Manning Clark's *'History of Australia'* - Volume One, and Robert Hughes *'Fatal Shore'*. Your local library should be able to provide you with other histories on the subject, if these books are not readily available in your area.
4. The recent High Court Mabo decision (wherein the earlier possession of parts of Australia by aborigines has now been judicially recognised at law by means of the concept of an inherent *native title*) has quite naturally qualified such earlier ceremonial claims for blanket possession. It will undoubtedly take many years of learned debate and perhaps statutory direction by Parliaments to clarify exactly what is now meant by the term *'native title'* and its attendant ramifications on current crown leases and undeveloped crown land held for and on behalf of the citizens of a particular Australian state.

- the Cyprus in full sail -

5. One public issue that appears prevalent in the reports of those times was the consistent demolishing 'over-night' by vandals of new picket fences, put up by landowning townsfolk in their early attempts to 'civilize' their newly acquired properties.
6. *Macquarie Harbour* was first established as a Penal Settlement in 1821. The original intent was to harvest the prominent stands of Huon pine for boat building purposes, and commence boat and ship building activities. During the period of occupation some notable world class brigs were constructed such as the *Cyprus* which was hi-jacked by convicts and taken to China via Tahiti, and the *Frederick* which was also hi-jacked and taken to Chile. Of the eleven that successfully escaped in the latter boat, four were recaptured some six years later and brought back to Hobart to stand trial. Their defence lawyer made a notable case out of their trial by successfully arguing that since the boat had not been completed or officially registered at the time of its theft, it was not a ship as such *'but a collection of timber'*, and therefore their charge of mutiny (which if convicted would have meant their hanging) was reduced. As a consequence the men were saved from the gallows and their sentences merely lengthened by several years! By the early 1830s the unsuitability of Macquarie Harbour had become apparent. The timber resource had now been exhausted, and there was low morale amongst the military stationed there. The sand bar at the harbour mouth was treacherous, and in adverse weather conditions it could take up to five weeks to get there by boat from Hobart Town. Apart from similar problems of distance and time to travel, Maria Island suffered from a different set of weaknesses. It was an easy place to escape from, and deemed to be not a tough enough environment to cater for the requirements of breaking the spirit of the 'incorrigibles'.

CHAPTER TWO

Laying the Foundations 1830-33

The history of Port Arthur as a place of correction for offenders falls naturally into several phases. In 1830 it started life simply as a Penal Settlement, for second offenders, the *incorrigibles*. However, it then grew in stature to serve at the leading edge in reformist philosophy. One pioneering feature was its wholesale segregation of the young boys from adult offenders at Point Puer. Another, was the construction of the *Model Separate Prison* in 1849, which was then considered to be one of the major corrective institutions of those times.

To appreciate fully Port Arthur's overall impact on both Tasmania and the British judicial system, it assists if we deal separately with each phase of its development and subsequent decline. This chapter commences the process by referring to the *Laying of Foundations* 1830-33.

Convicts and Commanders

During the first three year period the population of convicts at the Port Arthur Penal Settlement was to rise steadily to some 500 under sentence. The numbers of military personnel present rose to a little under 400. The first three Commandants (of what was viewed then as just another high security Penal Settlement), were military officers, but also practising doctors. Captain John Russell was the first Commandant, Captain John Mahon followed and then finally Lieutenant John Gibbons. All were officers of the British 63rd Regiment of Foot.

Like a Military Fiefdom

These Commandants had absolute authority over the entire Tasman Peninsula, and the area was treated as though it was a zone of military occupation. Any map of the district and your travel by road here today can only hint at how rough was the terrain in those days in an era before bulldozers, chainsaws, bitumen and high speed motor vehicles. It is an extremely large area, of some 500 square kilometres. The British Regiment's military annexation of such a large 'open air prison', has been regarded by some historians as being unique in the annals of Australia's colonial history.

What Life was Like in Those Days

A chain of dogs (mainly deer-hounds and mastiffs) were set up in a row of kennels one metre apart as an audible alarm system at the isthmus where Tasman Peninsula joins the mainland of Tasmania. This military post (Eaglehawk Neck), remained operational for the life of the Penal Settlement. It was reputed the guard dogs there were better fed than the convicts! The narrow sand-bar strip which is a feature of the 'Neck', was illuminated every night by means of kerosene lamps and guards patrolled the shore.

Existing records suggest that the detailed security arrangements in place at EagleHawk Neck (so vividly described below by a later Commandant of Port Arthur in January 1854), had changed little since the first years of settlement.

"..is only seventy-eight yards across...and double sentinels are posted day and night to prevent the ingress or egress of all unauthorised persons. A line of eighteen dogs also extends across the narrow isthmus, who, being constantly kept separate, are most ferocious, presenting on the approach of any stranger as vigilant a body of sentinels as it is possible to imagine; many of them have not been off the chain for years, and are consequently very savage.

Along the banks of the narrow strait which separates the two peninsulas detachments of armed constables are stationed at intervals, who being well rewarded for the apprehension of runaways, they are ever on the alert to prevent the convicts from swimming across."

- a sketch of Sir John and Lady Franklin visiting Eaglehawk Neck 1842 -
(COURTESY AUSTRALIAN NATIONAL LIBRARY)

At the Port Arthur Settlement itself, curfew was at dusk and all personnel needed a pass to be out at night. After the evening meal all convicts (whose daily rations at that time consisted of one and a half pounds of bread, half a pound of vegetables, a pound of salt meat and two ounces of salt), were locked up in their wooden barracks located near the military barracks on the hillside - beside and above where now stands the Commandant's house.

(COURTESY PORT ARTHUR COLLECTION)

Centipede Gangs

For a convict, the first six months after arrival consisted of common hard labour. This meant going out on work details known at Port Arthur as the *centipede gangs*. So named, because when carrying in the felled timber on their shoulders this long line of convicts moving in unison, took on the impression of being a huge human centipede.The sight of a hundred men all in a row dressed in rough prison garments, carrying a large tree on their shoulders, was an awesome sight not lost on the official visitor. Accidents did happen. A line of men could collapse like a pack of dominoes after the man in front stumbled; and human limbs were consequently squashed and broken, under the weight of a large tree obeying the forces of gravity.

The men on such work details were lightly shackled at the ankles to stop them absconding into the bush. However heavier irons were riveted on repeated offenders by the blacksmith, to serve as a specific punishment.

Type of Clothing Worn

The general convict was clothed in coarse hessian, black and yellow trousers and jacket which absorbed the rain like a sponge making the garb heavy and wet, and once wet the convict remained cold and the damp ate into his bones.

Yellow was the colour of humiliation and fashioned together with black resembled the traditional Court Jester or fool in society. Promotion was recognized by means of a change in uniform to that of a grey outfit. Such men were given positions of privilege, whereby their trades could be practised, and they were exempt from the rigours of hard labour.

Early Morning Rise

Just before first light a bell would be sounded. Upon rising each convict would be given half a pint of boiling water, and six ounces of course ground flour to be mixed together, to create a grey looking solution known as '*skilly*'. This hideous gruel would be drunk down as the morning sustenance. It was a policy to overwork, underfeed and inadequately clothe these individuals - to serve as retribution for their past misdeeds.

Governor George Arthur typifies the philosophy of such a penal process by making the following reference in official correspondence of this era:

'....*that within the bounds of humanity the offenders are to be subjected to the last degree of misery*'

Little Free Time

The convicts worked a five and a half day week, with Saturday afternoons off to clean their clothes, and wash themselves. There was some component of free time which could comprise cultivating a small vegetable garden, though this could be denied them as part of the punishment process.

On Sunday the Sabbath was marked by compulsory church attendance in the morning, followed by free time later in the day.

Discipline and the Use of the Cat-o-Nine Tails

Because this early period was under strict military discipline, the slightest breach of rules and regulations resulted in charges for the offender followed by Summary punishment. There were levels of severity, which related directly to the nature of the offence committed, and privileges were likewise closely monitored.

In the presence of all prisoners, physical sentences such as flogging with the cat-o-nine tails, would be inflicted upon absconders. The standard rank and file of the military were also required to attend to observe the spectacle.

When such an event took place, a certain parade etiquette was observed to maximise the full effect of the occasion. The procedures were also designed to reinforce in the minds of the convicts, the realities of the absolute control held over them by their gaolers.

Treatment of Absconders

Absconders were tied to the infamous 'triangle', which was openly referred to as the *altar of discipline*, and could expect to receive up to one hundred lashes which would reduce a man's back to an oozing mass of raw flesh.

Should an absconder faint in the course of the flogging, it was Standing Orders that he be revived in a shallow *salt bath* located nearby. The provision of such a bath was not simply part of the ritual to allow the balance of the sentence to be completed, but also to maximise the horror of the experience, and thus vividly reinforce the deterrent effect on observers. A doctor was always present, and should he form the view that the life of the convict was in jeopardy, had the power to stop the completion of the sentence.

Such spectacles were normally reserved to a Sunday morning and once over, all assembled were then marched off ....to "*Praise the Lord*". The offender was normally given the next forty-eight hours off work after receiving the flogging, and then, after leg-irons were fitted, assigned to work in the salt water at the boat-yard, to help heal the wounds on their back.

- contemporary sketch showing the location of the Isle of the Dead cemetery and Point Puer across the bay -
(COURTESY PORT ARTHUR COLLECTION)

Isle of the Dead

The little island you can observe at the edge of the bay, is referred to locally as the Isle of the Dead. It was first used as a burial ground for the settlement in February 1833. Reverend John A. Morton, a Wesleyan Missionary who specialised in ministering to convicts (and had previously served at the Macquarie Harbour Penal Settlement), arrived at Port Arthur to take up duties there on the 19th April 1833. He subsequently wrote the following short tract :

"*In the spacious bay, on the verge of which the settlement is situated, at the distance of a mile, stands a lovely little island, about a half a mile in circumference at the water's edge. This it appeared to me, would be a secure undisturbed resting place, where the departed prisoners might lie together until the morning of the resurrection...no stone marks whereabouts he slumbers, as no tombstones or other mark is allowed to be placed at the head of the graves.*"

- contemporary photographs taken either shortly before or after closure of the Prison. (Above) are the convict graves with no headstones to mark each individuals resting place, while (Below) are those of free persons -
(COURTESY TASMANIAN FILM CORPORATION)

(COURTESY TASMANIAN FILM CORPORATION)

The bodies of some 1,769 convicts lie buried there with no tombstone to mark each grave site. In direct contrast there are also located there (with tombstones originally placed to mark the graves), the remains of some 81 free persons; being mainly soldiers, warders and their families who died due to sickness, accident or misadventure. Of the latter graves approximately seventy-six headstones remain, with many requiring urgent maintenance.

Being a solitary and sombre task, the duties of grave digger during the forty-seven years of the Penal Settlement's existence, were normally given, to the social outcasts within the prison system itself: those convicts guilty of offences against children.

A Change in Stature
Captain Charles O'Hara Booth, of the 21st Fusiliers (1), who had served previously in India, the West Indies, South America, St Vincent and Ireland arrived in Hobart Town on the 1st of February 1833. Within six weeks of his arrival he was appointed as the next Commandant of Port Arthur and arrived there on the 16th March 1833. As Chapter Three will reveal, O'Hara Booth heralded in a new phase of the development of Port Arthur. Under his eleven year stewardship the status of Port Arthur would change from being simply that of a remote Penal Settlement, to one of His Majesty's foremost Imperial Prisons.

Footnotes:
1. A 'fusil' was a special type of light musket used by some British Infantry Regiments at that time. The soldiers who exclusively used the weapon were called "Fusiliers" To distinguish one group of soldiers from another, each Regiment had their own unique Regimental number as well: e.g. 21st Fusiliers.

- Charles O'Hara Booth in military ceremonial dress as painted by his friend Thomas Lempriere -
(COURTESY PORT ARTHUR COLLECTION)

- the dress uniform of a Private of the 99th Regiment of Foot in 1845 -

CHAPTER THREE

Consolidation 1834-44

Increasing numbers of convicts were now to come to Port Arthur from a variety of backgrounds: not simply 'lifers' serving long sentences or incorrigible second offenders, but tradesmen, architects, professionals, political activists, and a new wave of convicts subsequently referred to in the Justice system, as juvenile offenders.

Arrival of Convict boys at Port Arthur - 1834

This latter group, of young boys convicted in the main of petty theft, transferred from Hobart Town for the first time in January 1834. These boys, as a sectional group had developed an infamous reputation in Hobart Town.

- Charles O'Hara Booth in mufti -

We know from Governor Arthur's correspondence he did not hold the boys in high regard: *'entirely useless and generally so mischievous are these corrupt little rogues that they are the dread of every family'*

The background to the decision to route these boys direct to Port Arthur stemmed from the fact that by 1833, those arriving on previous convict ships, had created a major administrative problem for the local authorities. After a series of incidents involving mischievous behaviour by these boy convicts, resistance amongst the free families progressed to such an extent that they were now unwilling to take them on assignment.

Given that the Juvenile Section at the Carter Barracks in Sydney, had only recently been closed down because of perceived disciplinary shortcomings, then Governor Arthur had no option but to seek a new solution to this emerging social problem. On the one hand he faced civic pressures that these delinquents now arriving be located at some distance from the main free settlement areas, yet on the other they needed to be housed in a disciplined environment so that they might learn meaningful skills. The solution was that they be sent on to the Port Arthur Penal Settlement.

- early painting by Richard Newman of Point Puer as seen across the bay from the Commandant's garden -
(COURTESY PORT ARTHUR COLLECTION)

Point Puer

The Governor had approved Booth's Plan in December 1833 to set up a dormitory complex and school at Point Puer across the bay from the main Port Arthur settlement. The first Superintendent was a retiree from the 63rd Regiment John Montgomery, whose propensity to drink alcoholic beverages had cut short his military career.

The first group of boys to arrive did so with great *panache* and *style*. There were 68 in the first consignment and they came off the brig transport *Tamar* at Port Arthur on the 10th January 1834 intoxicated, having successfully broken into a wine supply on board, the contents of which had been previously destined to be delivered to the Commandant!

With the establishment of the buildings and dormitories at Point Puer, Port Arthur now became the destination for all young boys sentenced to transportation to Australia. The first purpose-designed 'young offenders' convict ship was called the **Frances Charlotte**. Over the next few years, it was destined to be the first of eight juvenile ships plying their way between Portsmouth and Van Diemen's Land.

During the period 1838-1841, 1200 boy convicts aged between the ages of 10 and 18 arrived and were either assigned as domestic servants or went to Point Puer. By 1836 the numbers of boys housed at Point Puer had risen to 280, and by 1838 some 375 were located there. By 1843, which was at the height of its use, there were close to 800 boys present at the time when Benjamin Horne, their Headmaster, was conducting a general review of their contemporary welfare, education and training practices.

Through their respective age and size groupings the boys were also subcategorised into three classes of behaviour: a *general* class open to privileges, a *confined* class, and a *punishment* class.

Daily Routine

The daily routine for the boys (which was criticised by Benjamin Horne in his 132 page report as being -too lax), is best described by the following extract taken from the earlier evidence of the Commandant Charles O'Hara Booth, given to the Select Committee on Transportation in 1837 :

"...rising at 5 a.m., roll up and stow their hammock bedding, whole are assembled together, a portion of scripture and a suitable morning prayer is read by the catechist after which the boys leave the barracks, wash and amuse themselves within the prescribed bounds (extending to about a quarter of a mile), preparatory as to be inspected for personal cleanliness prior to breakfast which takes place at 7 oclock, the meal ended they again dispersed until the general muster for the labours of the day commencing at eight o'clock. They continue to work until noon. They are then obliged to prepare and wash themselves previous to another inspection for personal cleanliness, and dinner is at half-past twelve. The boys are divided into messes of ten or twelve each. Corporals are appointed one for each mess. At a quarter past six the boys are mustered for school, which continues one hour when the evening is closed by singing the evening hymn. A portion of scripture is read as in the morning after which the boys retire to bed, and lights are kept burning in the barracks and a watch is kept by overseers alternatively during the night.

On the question of punishment, the most trivial crime or irregularity is not permitted to pass without punishment in proportion to the nature or degree of the offence, which consists of confinement to the muster ground after labour where no amusement is allowed and the boys are required to do the duty of scavengers. The next grade of punishment for the more refractory spirit is to have the boy placed in a punishment cell where no talking or noise is permitted and they receive their meals therein. The next grade of punishment is in the cell on bread and water. In cases of more determined violation of the regulations the offender is sentenced to punishment on the breech. This measure is never resorted to until every other means of reform have been resorted to without effect. The maximum being 36 lashes."

While by no means comprehensive, the trades the boys were allowed to engage in were carpentry, shoe making, tailoring, baking, gardening, bookbinding, and turning. The older boys were allowed stone-cutting, brick making, and boat-building along with blacksmith work and coopering. Their dress was also different from the rank and file. It was the grey of the trusted convict, as against the yellow and black of the hardened felon.

The Missionary James Backhouse paid a visit to Port Arthur in November 1834 and made the following comments concerning the housing of the boys at Point Puer, which suggests on close reading that perhaps it was the convict carpenters at Port Arthur that invented the term - multifunctional!

"*The boys' barracks is so constructed as to answer as a dormitory, as well as for the dining room and the school-room. The desks are all along the middle of the room: they let down when not wanted, and when required for a table are brought to a level, by bringing out the brackets under the wedge shaped attachments to the under sides of the leaves. The boys sleep in hammocks: which are suspended on hooks fixed in beams along the wall, and in others fit into notches in uprights along the central part of the room, which also support shelves on which the hammocks, when rolled up are placed: the movable beams are then fixed as fronts to the shelves.*"

Contemporary recorders of those times perceived the Point Puer system to be 'an oasis in the desert of penal government'. In reality though, the boys who were transported to Tasmania were very much street-wise and vicious behaviour at times did occur. The hospitalisation and near death of at least one highly disliked overseer, is recorded.

Consolidation of Industry

1. Boat building: Since it was a logistic necessity to have a boatyard servicing such a remote area, Port Arthur soon developed a comprehensive boat building industry during the period 1833-44. With more and more convicts arriving with related skills and surrounded by copious quantities of raw materials, the humble boat-repair facility blossomed into a major ship-building concern where the heaviest ships in Australia were to be manufactured until the mid 1840s. After that, competing private enterprise pressures from Hobart, and scandals as to the on-selling of newly constructed brigs by private agents, forced its demise (1).

- *the barque **Lady Franklin** -*
(COURTESY TASMANIAN MUSEUM AND ART GALLERY)

The boat-building industry first took off in meaningful form when the settlement engaged a free shipwright, John Watson. Mr Watson ran the boatyard between 1833-1837, and was then replaced by David Hoy. Mr Hoy ran the boatyard until its final closure in 1849. Readers will recall that Mr Hoy had several years earlier been a victim of the *Frederick* hi-jack from Macquarie Harbour (2). Many three-masted ocean-going tall ships were built at the yard during its productive life, with some weighing in excess of 250 tons (3).

Apart from large vessels, a multitude of small whale and rowing boats were constructed, as well as tugs for the coal mines and buoys

- Shipwright's Cottage located close to the shore overlooking the boatyard -
(COURTESY TASMANIAN MUSEUM AND ART GALLERY)

for navigational assistance. Returns for 1837 revealed that more than 80 boats were constructed in that fiscal year and we believe further primary resource historical research will reveal that earlier assumptions made by some historians as to the productivity of the yard, have been unduly conservative.

2. Supporting Trades: Sail making, cabinet making, coopering, wheel-wrights, and smithing, were some of the trades on site directly supporting the boat building activities at Port Arthur at this time. Other flourishing trades were stone masonry, brick making, lime burning (manufacture of cement from sea-shells), along with timber industry trades, such as the production of shingles for roofs, stud framing, and palings for fences.

All represented an important raw construction industry. For instance, production levels of the order of 68,000 hand-made bricks per month, seemed to be maintained for at least a decade! Such a diversity of manufacturing for the colony provided an important cashflow for the military Treasury Chest of the day. The value to the colony of the convict workforce located at Port Arthur during this period is best symbolised by the fact that even the foundation stones for Government House, Hobart, were quarried and fashioned at Port Arthur.

3. Mining of Coal: On the north side of the Peninsula, some four hours horse-ride away from the Prison, rich coal seams were discovered, and consequently over a period of 14 months, with only picks and shovels to aid them, convicts drove a shaft some 100 metres (300 feet) deep. This new industry whereby coal was extracted manually by the convicts to fuel hearths in Hobart Town, was not only much cheaper to buy than that previously shipped in from Newcastle, New South Wales, but also allowed the colony to be self-sufficient in this regard.

The coal, however, had its own special burning qualities. It had the dramatic reputation for exploding in the fire-place! Even so, it was eagerly consumed by the townsfolk of Hobart, with production in the order of 250 tons a week in 1842! What makes these production figures even more remarkable, is that the work was all done by hard manual labour, and without animal assistance.

- view from the Prison Dairy Farm -
(COURTESY PORT ARTHUR COLLECTION)

4. *Agriculture:* Agriculture was also flourishing during this period to the point that the Tasman Peninsula was self-sufficient in food. Again it needs to be appreciated how this was done. There were no oxen, or horses involved. Men were yoked up like human cattle (14 in a team), to plough the fields.

At least *twelve separate crops* were produced; potatoes, carrots, turnips, parsnips, leeks, swede, peas, cabbage, wheat, barley, salad produce, and hay including seed for the following year's crop. To serve as but one example, in 1845 101,000 lbs of cabbage alone was produced at the Port Arthur farm, while the outstation at Impression Bay produced 37 tons of potatoes.

Convict Department returns for agricultural produce during the period, list prison farms at 'Impression Bay', 'Saltwater River', 'Coal Mines', 'Wedge Bay', 'Cascades', 'Point Puer', and Port Arthur itself. A release of deer at 'Sloping Main', provided *sporting recreation* for the military, and the dairy farm at Port Arthur was located next to where the Model Prison now stands.

5. *Clothing and Furniture:* Clothing and furniture was made for the convict department of the British Colonial Office. Personal attire for the military often created incentives for tradesmen under sentence in their spare time. They would be paid either with contraband, such as plugs of tobacco, tea and sugar, or a financial reward serving as credits for their final release. A trusted cobbler could earn in the order of a shilling a week from the authorities. Such practices were accepted as beneficial, in that they provided inmates with a lump sum on release and helped cushion the realities of possible destitution.

Pressures on Health

Such hard manual labour productivity, was not without cost in terms of the health pressures endured by convicts. It is worthwhile therefore if we pause for a moment and consider the level of training received by the doctors who were now being recruited to serve at this remote outpost of the British penal system.

On the main they came from the British training colleges, with some having served as shipboard surgeons on convict transports. In the first three decades of the nineteenth century, major advances had been made in medical science. Doctors were no longer the carpenter doubling as a 'saw-bones' on the sailing ships, and their professional standing in the community had been regularised by a British Act of Parliament. The need for such an Act had in part been brought on by the political furore raised at that time due to the prevalence of grave robbing - previously defended as being in the interests of the advancement of medical science!

During this period of consolidation at Port Arthur (1834-44), and with Captain O'Hara Booth not being a practising doctor, these recruited doctors became (reflecting the diversity of the skills they were called upon to practice in the Prison and on the Peninsula), the Commandant's Second-in-Command.

- photograph of the front of the hospital taken in the late 1800s before the great 1895/97 bushfires -
(COURTESY PORT ARTHUR COLLECTION)

Hospital Services

One of the most imposing buildings on site today even though very much a ruin (due to bushfires in 1895 and 1897), is the hospital. It was completed in 1842, and its architect was the convict Henry Lang (4). This brick and sandstone (quarried at Point Puer) monument, had replaced the first hospital, which was a much smaller wooden building previously located just below it on the hill.

As the above photograph and on the page following clearly show, there were two upper and lower wards located in separate wings of the building . They were capable of caring for up to 80 patients. This medical centre was staffed by one doctor aided by trusted convicts who had been assigned to act as medical orderlies.

Hospital - Port Arthur

This imposing side photograph of the hospital (Courtesy Tasmanian Museum and Art Gallery), also clearly shows the doorway arch inset into the substantial brick retaining wall. This side entrance led to the kitchen, toilets and mortuary which were below ground level. It also provides us with a good view of Smith O'Brien's cottage (whose activities are referred to a little later) at the top right, and in the foreground bottom right is the Invalid's Mess Hall, which at times doubled as an Entertainment Hall for the guards and visiting notaries.

Hospital services in those days were not aided by the wonder drugs of today. There was neither anaesthetic nor anti-bacterial drugs of note such as penicillin. Surgery was very much a rough and ready affair, with the likelihood of a fatal infection for even the most minor of operations.

Diversity of Duties
The workload for the Resident medical officer was very large at this time. Not only did his responsibilities extend to those located in the Port Arthur settlement itself (the convicts, the soldiers, the warders and their wives and children), but also the Tasman Peninsula as a whole. Medicines in general were in short supply, with items such as bandages having to compete with other non-medical needs on site in terms of the overall budget.

Also, much frustration was no doubt felt by successive medical officers as to an inherent conflict in their duties. On the one hand they had a never ending stream of general practice matters to attend to (e.g. the birth of a child on a distant outstation), while on the other as the Prison doctor they might be required to attend, as a matter of protocol endless inspection visits of a routine nature. Such inspections being requested by the military, to ensure there was no malingering amongst the convicts. In the wards, the convict boys, soldiers and warders were kept separate from the rank and file convicts, while the more senior prison staff and their families were attended to in their homes.

Being a very physical labour-orientated existence in those days, with an environment of long bouts of dampness in winter (not assisted by the type of clothes worn by the convicts), it was no surprising that the sickness and accident cases requiring medical attention in the early 1840s - when the settlement was at its busiest - were recorded at a very high level. Some 30 to 40 new cases recorded each day for this period was not unusual. Respiratory complaints and broken limbs, from working on the timber gangs, were common.

Availability of Fresh Food

While earlier informed commentaries about Port Arthur have highlighted the dramatic side of i history, such as the floggings and the hard labour associated with the coal mines or timber getting activities, it should be equally appreciated that the quality and quantity of fresh food made avail to the convicts, was superior in kind to that they may have received had they remained in the industrial squalor of the English manufacturing towns, from which they had been transported.

The Molesworth Select Committee's findings (5) in the late 1830s noted that the tradesmen at Fort Arthur under sentence, had a better diet than the free agricultural workers of England.

The Effect of Ameliorating Conditions:

By 1838 it was recognized by the authorities (with some measure of disdain), that the Molesworth Select Committee findings provided clear evidence that because of the improved conditions at Port Arthur - Transportation was 'no longer a sufficient deterrent'. This assessment (when combined with the collateral finding that in remote locations there was no way of effectively monitoring convict household assignments in a just manner), heralded major changes in '. policy back in England.

The first major change in direction was that the transportation of convicts from England to the mainland of Australia under the assignment system, was stopped in 1840. In its place a **Probationary System** was introduced which only applied to Van Diemen's Land. From now on only V.D.L. was to exclusively receive convicts. This practice was destined to continue for the next 13 years.

Such a monopoly of human cargo 'under probation' for the period 1840-53 is the root cause why, in the final analysis, Tasmania received approximately 50% of all convicts despatched from England and other Imperial posts (6), to serve time in the Antipodes.

One of the most colourful individuals of this period to be transported and incarcerated at Port Arthur, was *Linus Miller*. Mr Miller was a native of New York City, America. He was a lawyer by profession who had been arrested at the Niagara Falls as the outspoken advocate for the 1837 Rebellion of Upper Canada (Ontario).

This young and very tall American, shortly after arrival, suffered ill-health as a direct result of being part of the centipede gangs. Then, having been hospitalised for several weeks his erudite sk lls came to the fore and he ended up being a *tutor* to some of the officers' children! Perhaps his sentencing judge would not have seen the humour of a man he had found convicted of high treason for seditious thoughts, being placed in a position of trust and authority over the young developing minds of the children of his gaolers!

The Prison Matures in Stature

With the maturing of the site by 1837 there was a qualitative change in the administration of the day to day activities. Charles O'Hara Booth had now sold his military commission, and was acting as a 'Civil' as against Military Commandant. Wives and daughters of officials were becoming a more prominent feature of the social landscape, though kept strictly apart from the routine fabric of discipline at the prison.

In 1838 the Commandant married Elizabeth Charlotte Eagle, the step-daughter of Booth's Regimental Surgeon and subsequently they raised several children at the settlement, prior to his resignation due to ill health in 1844.

- the Government Gardens with its central fountain was a major feature -
(COURTESY ARCHIVES OFFICE OF TASMANIA)

The ameliorating influence of women folk now took an overt form, with the harshness of the environs softened to please them with the planting out of English trees (with oaks, elms and ash (7) being in preponderance), and rose gardens to create some vestiges of the familiarity of their homeland. Even blackbirds were introduced in the late 1830s to provide familiar birdsong.

In turn more refined social gatherings were now encouraged to assist in making life appear less onerous for the wives and children of the prison authorities, even though constant calls for improved housing conditions for families, appeared to fall on deaf ears!

Religious Matters
Construction of the church at Port Arthur commenced in 1835, and took eleven months to build. The architect was the convict Henry Lang. During its construction a murder took place amongst the convicts and the perpetrator of the crime was hanged in Hobart. The church building located prominently on the hill (and which the visitor observes to their right screened by English trees as they first enter the site), was the first major permanent structure of stone to be built at Port Arthur. The church was originally constructed with thirteen spires. However, after concerns were raised on this subject by Lady Jane Franklin, the wife of the Governor who replaced Governor Arthur in 1837, a wooden 14th spire was added. The main spire was approximately 33 metres high, as shown in the photograph opposite. It was made of wood painted to look like stone. It was incidentally Lady Jane Franklin, who was particularly partial to the gothic style churches of her European upbringing, who in correspondence to a friend described the Port Arthur church as 'a rather squat and ugly building' - apparently it was not 'gothic' enough for her! As it turned out the 14th spire was later blown down in high winds in 1876, and never replaced.

When completed, the church boasted a bell tower which housed a peal of eight bells. All had been cast at Port Arthur in the prison foundry, which was located next to the large granary building on the foreshore.

- this attractive main entrance to the church was the preserve for officers, soldiers, and their families -
(COURTESY TASMANIAN MUSEUM AND ART GALLERY)

The first religious service was held in the constructed church in 1837. However because of sectarian rivalry it was never consecrated (Wesleyans had used it first then it was taken over by the Anglicans), even though regular church services were held there every Sunday. It was capable of seating up to 1,000 convicts, with additional accommodation for 200 officials.

While outside the scope of this short history, it should be mentioned a fire in February 1884 destroyed the roof, and left the church in ruins (8).

Communications and Transport
The basic principles of the semaphore system (reputedly invented by a clergyman and first used in the Channel Islands in the English Channel and then improved by a Sir Hugh Popham), was used in the Sydney Town area and then followed by localised use in the Derwent and D'Entrecasteaux Channel areas of Van Diemen's Land.

Captain O'Hara Booth, shortly after his arrival in late 1833 saw the value of the system for the Peninsula and not long afterwards a row of semaphore stations were in place enabling messages to be sent from Port Arthur to Hobart Town in a matter of some 20 minutes.

First Major Tramway in Australia
In technological terms the Tasman Peninsula under Captain O'Hara Booth also led the times in transport systems. Port Arthur convicts under his stewardship set up the first long distance passenger tramway system in Australia. Established and operational in 1836, it also carried vital supplies for the Settlement.

The tramway was approximately 6 kilometres long, and commencing at Norfolk Bay (Taranna), wound its way to Long Bay (Oakwood). From there the supplies were conveyed by vessel on sheltered waters to the quay at Port Arthur. A feature of the railroad was that the rails were made of wood, as well as the base being constructed of wooden sleepers set one foot apart, with the ballast made up of sand or clay.

- one of the chain of semaphore stations which used to link the Tasman Peninsula with Hobart -

- contemporary sketch of the tramway in operation -
(COURTESY PORT ARTHUR COLLECTION)

Mishaps were not infrequent since at times on the down slopes the carriage could reach speeds of up to 50 kilometres per hour and tip-ups did occur. At least one visiting Colonial Secretary (James Bicheno) was catapulted unceremoniously, complete in finery, into the bushes! Visiting officials were also fair game for the convicts who propelled this unique carriage. The convicts frequently used the opportunity, when dusting down their charges, to practise their well worn pick-pocket skills!

During the 1840s with the expansion of the mining of coal at Saltwater River, and the getting of timber from the adjacent probation stations, an iron-rail railway was laid onto the jetty there for the onforwarding by sea of such heavily weighted commercial material.

Role and Conditions for Convict Women:

Of the total complement of 778 persons who arrived under sentence with the First Fleet in 1788, one hundred and ninety two were women. The majority had been sent out for petty theft, with less than 4% of those transported convicted for prostitution. In the First Fleet there was a mix of the sexes, but in later despatches the sexes were segregated with principally either male or female transportation vessels sent out; but of course in both instances the crews on the boats were male. On the female ships there was some measure of fraternisation between the crew and soldiers and their human cargo, which was against the rules, but in many cases over-looked. The occasional scandal did emerge, but circumstances were more complex than might at first appear e.g. a woman might chose to have close associations with a particular soldier as a precarious form of protection against the unwanted advances from other quarters.

Assigned convict women employed as servants were exposed to sexual harassment and rape from their employers, and many had no option but to tolerate the 'status quo' as a pragmatic trade-off for the basics of life such as shelter, food and a place to sleep.

STATISTICAL MINUTES of the Boys' Establishment, Poi

MONTHS.	Strength at end of month.	Received from Hobart Town.	Discharged to Hobart Town.	Received from Port Arthur.	Discharged to Port Arthur.	Deaths.	EDUCATION ON LANDING.					Trade and Number of Days E		
							Could Cypher.	Read and Write.	Read.	Could not Read.	Learned to read since.	Carpenters. 7s. p.w.	Sawyers. 10s. p.w.	Tailors. 4s. p.w.
January	238						21	55	132	106	105	721	790	698
February	221	1	13	7	11	1	17	35	111	110	110	496	458	445
March	214	1			8		18	35	107	107	107	530	319	346
April	177		4		33		18	33	92	85	85	503	586	328
May	278	141	12		29		34	57	179	98	58	553	436	542
June	273	2		2	8		34	56	174	99	58	604	616	320
TOTALS.		145	29	9	89	1						3,407	3,205	2,679

er, Tasman's Peninsula, for the Half Year ending 30/6/1837.

Gangs: in each Month.			VALUE OF LABOUR	Timber Cut.	Vegetables Raised.		VALUE OF VEGETABLES	REMARKS.
Shoemakers.	Gardeners.	Labourers.			Potatoes, 1 d. per lb.	Cabbages and Turnips, ½ d. per lb.		
5s. p.w.	2s. p.w.	2s. p.w.						
			Ł. s. d.	Feet.	lbs.	lbs.	Ł. s. d.	
1,747	174	2,864	224 13 8	11,702		1,769	3 13 8½	
1,380	126	3,158	172 1 1	7,720	3,189½	328	14 13 1½	
1,513	90	3,301	179 6 6	4,167	3,062½	844	14 10 4½	
1,273	142	2,480	169 13 5	7,642	11,245½	1,037	49 - 4	
1,315	198	2,991	177 3 9	6,130	2,723	1,710	14 18 2	
1,323	272	4,453	212 1 2	10,227	1,482	1,220	8 14 4	
8,551	1,002	19,247	1134 19 7	46,988	21,702½	6,908	115 10 -½	

(signed) *Charles O'Hara Booth, Comm.*

Quite unfairly, it was often the woman that received punishment for the detection of such liaisons (9); especially if unwanted pregnancy was the result. Not only would they then have to return to the Female factory, where employment opportunities would be lost, but they might suffer public humiliation in terms of having their head shaved, or a steel collar (like that one might place around the neck of a dog) to serve as part of their sentence: for some past sexual act that more often than not had been without their consent and beyond their physical control. No convicted women were ever sent to Port Arthur as a convict. However some did arrive there as assigned domestic servants for the families of the administration, during the consolidation phase.

Booth's Achievements in Retrospect

A measuring of Booth's achievements, is best appreciated by understanding that at the time of his departure in 1844 there would be some 1200 adult convicts and of the order of 800 boy convicts located on site, and when the families of the military and administration is added (some 900 all told), it can be seen that this concentration of some 3,000 Europeans at Port Arthur made it unofficially the *second largest settlement of Europeans in Van Diemen's Land* at that time. Only the town of Hobart boasted a greater number of people.

Indeed the granary building (which today is the remaining largest ruin to be observed on site), serves as a tangible monument to the diversity and scale of industry then operating at Port Arthur at that time. It was in fact the largest single brick and stone structure of its kind in Australia, when completed in 1844 (10). The Tasman Peninsula as a whole was supporting a population of just under seven thousand people, three-quarters of whom were under sentence. This population grouping then represented *some 10% of the total population of the island.*

It is a sad reflection therefore, that the colonial bureaucracy were extremely unkind to their most talented and highly regarded public servant Charles O'Hara Booth. Not only did they fail to provide him with his own horse to carry out his duties as Commandant, and hence had to purchase his own (11) but when ill health, suffered in the line of duty (12), forced him to retire in 1843 (followed by his early death in 1851 (13)), his young family was left virtually destitute and faced the likely prospect for a time of being removed to the Poor House. A rather tragic end to the family of a man who had faithfully served King and Country, since the age of sixteen.

Photograph to the left is the portrait of happy times for the Booths. A social function at Stoke House Newtown, which became their family residence after leaving Port Arthur, and before Charles Booth's unfortunate heart attack on the 11th August 1851.Charlotte his wife, who was nearly half his age, had no option but to leave Tasmania almost destitute in 1852. She sailed to England with her daughters to seek a widow's pension from the British army. Her mission was unsuccessful, but Charlotte found work as a boarding school Matron and was the ripe age of 84 when she died in 1903.

Footnotes:

1. A scandal received prominence in mid 1842 concerning the building of a steamship for a private company owned by a Captain Swanston. The bottom line was the steamship had been constructed by the Port Arthur boatyards for a charge of some 350 pounds based on the convict rate of pay, when at the normal commercial rate it should have cost 2,500 pounds. Furthermore, Swanston's company turned around shortly afterwards and sold the boat interstate (admittedly the cost of the steam engines and associated equipment had been a separate item), for 7,000 pounds!

The inestimable value of the Port Arthur boatyards at that time cannot be understated. What few may appreciate is that the ability to repair boats was just as important as the ability to construct new ones. The wear and tear on the existing vessels, given that sea travel was a major feature of those times, was at times horrific, quite apart from the lives lost due to nautical misadventure.

For example in a four week period (August/September 1842), not only did the Lady Franklin, run aground near the Hippolyte Rocks damaging her hull, but managed to limp back to Port Arthur (with ten feet of water in her holds) to be repaired, but within the fortnight the supply ship the Isabella struck a reef on the north side of Betsy Island. The sailors, having thrown over-board her consignment of some 3,200 bricks, and offloaded the convicts at the Coal Mines, were then able to have her speedily repaired and brought back into service again. The effective skil-ls-resource base, built up during O'Hara Booth's time at Port Arthur, was of incalculable value to the fledgling colony. His competency as a sound planner and careful administrator was widely appreciated.

2. David Hoy had been marooned with minimal supplies with other warders at Macquarie Har-bour when the escapees took the Frederick. They were left with only a small dinghy and it took them 10 days to raise the alarm. Hoy sought compensation from the government for hardship suffered and was a principal witness regarding the prosecution of the mutineers when four were recaptured off the coast of Chile, and brought back to Hobart for trial.

3. The Elisa of 146 tons was built in 1835, the barque Fanny was built in 1837 and was at that time (at 237 tons) the biggest ship built in the colony . The Lady Franklin built in 1842 was 286 tons and plied a regular route between Hobart Town and Norfolk Island in the Pacific, carrying sup-plies and convicts. In 1858 it joined the whaling fleet and was renamed the Emily Downing. Other ships of note built were the Eleanor, and the steel hulled paddle-steamer The Derwent.

4. Henry Lang was the convict architect responsible. He also designed and was overseer for the construction of the church. In the 1850s several additional facilities were built close by. First a separate morgue was constructed, and then a wash-house. It is a quirk of fate that the building is not standing on site today, fully restored. Two bushfires, one in January 1895, and the other in December 1897 left the building unrepairable: the outer walls having been dangerously weak-ened by the intensity of heat of those fires. This frustrated the intended plans of the Roman Catholic church (who had bought this imposing building subsequent to the closure of the pris-on), to use it as an educational college for boys. An unfortunate end to an historic building which earlier had fulfilled an important function for the community at large.

5. The Select Committee on Transportation, headed by Sir William Molesworth, was set up to review the fairness of the 'Assignment system'. It reported back to the British Parliament in late 1838. Its findings were that the system of assignment was defective and recommended its im-mediate discontinuance. In its place the suggestion made was for a Separate Penitentiary System of imprisonment as was then operating in America. The Model mentioned (although the extra expense of operation was fully appreciated), was the Albury State Prison in New York State.

6. Port Arthur had by now received convicts from as far a field as Hong Kong to Canada, and Capetown to Corfu.

7. Many of these trees still grace the site today to the extent that some tourists find their presence to be one of the most memorable features of their visit.

8. A Port Arthur Historic Site Information Pamphlet (Notes No.17) provides visitors with an update on conservation programmes effected to stabilize its structure as a historic ruin, from that time to the present day.

9. There is the interesting profile of an Anne Forest from County Cork Ireland, who was assigned to the Lampriere family, and on occasion, because of her wayward nature and in coming in after dark 'smelling of rum and military', was punished by being given ' a month at the wash tubs'.

10. It has been estimated that over 1,000,000 handmade convict bricks went into its construction, all of which had been made on site.

11. Indeed initially not only had Booth been forced to purchase his horse from his own means, but it took several years for him to convince the convict department that he, as Commandant, was rightfully entitled to a forage allowance for the beast!

12. He had in the course of a field visit in mid 1838 to an outstation, become lost on the impenetrable Forestier's Peninsula. He was not found for three days and suffered severe exposure as a result. His health never appeared to really recover from this ordeal. It is alleged it was one of his faithful dogs that saved his life on that day, by leading the searchers to him, he being too weak and frostbitten to call out himself.

13. Booth then took up the position of Principal of the Queen's Orphanage at Newtown, until his early death in August 1851.

- *the 146 tons schooner Elisa was completed in 1835 at the Port Arthur boatyards and was the forerunner of a line of beautiful sailing barques and brigs constructed during Captain O'Hara Booth's tenure as Commandant at Port Arthur -*
(COURTESY TASMANIAN MUSEUM AND ART GALLERY)

CHAPTER FOUR
Holding the Line 1844-48

With Charles O'Hara Booth seeking to resign in 1843 due to ill health (1), Major F. Mainwaring served as Acting Commandant from the 1st of January 1844, until Mr William Thomas Champ JP was officially appointed the new Commandant and took up residence there, on the 30th March 1844.

William Thomas Napier Champ JP
The new Commandant was a man of a very different style. William Thomas Napier Champ had a military background, but his main credentials were those of a travelling magistrate. In terms of status Port Arthur was now no longer simply a penal settlement, but that of an established Imperial Prison.

One of the first matters on Champ's agenda for action was to consider Benjamin Horne's Report on Point Puer which was forwarded to him for consideration in June. Horne had died on the 26th October the previous year, of tuberculosis. Horne's recommendations in the main were that the site was unsuitable, and proposed the relocation of the boys to Maria Island. On the grounds of the cost of re-location the Maria Island option was discounted, with Champ considering the alternative option of Safety Cove. As events unfolded, no overt action was taken to deal with the identified problems for another five years.

- William Thomas Napier Champ JP -
(COURTESY TASMANIAN MUSEUM ART GALLERY)

Steady as We Go
The next four years were essentially a 'steady as we go' administration, with convicts now arriving from England, not stained as *sentenced* men in the vogue so vividly depicted in Marcus Clarke's novel *'For the Term of his Natural Life'*, but rather as *probationers* (1).

In Van Diemen's Land (Tasmania), a groundswell of discontent as a result of the continued import of convicts, was fermenting, particularly in the north of the colony. It was led by the Reverend John West and James Aikenhead, the Editor of the **Launceston Examiner**. Their cause was the abolition of Transportation. Their association was named the Anti-Transportation League, whose logo subsequently became *Australia's National Flag*.

Implementation of New Penal Philosophies
Further afield, prison reformers based in London had established a new penal institution at Pentonville in 1842. It was loosely based on Bentham's **Panopticon**, designed in the late eighteenth century for the criminal, mentally ill, and even intractable delinquents. It's rehabilitation philosophy was based on a procedure that each prisoner was isolated, numerically identified, and under permanent surveillance (without them having direct knowledge of such observation), and that through such a process *modifications in behaviour* to the offender could be achieved in reforming *their basic character*. The postulated aim was to turn them away from ungodly acts and towards playing a productive role in society. Pentonville was to serve as the new model for all future prison systems.

On the page following is a curious document of those times drafted as a form of *Notice*, which makes it clear, to Pentonville inmates in London that the very worst of convicts -*'Prisoners who have behaved ill'*- will be accorded Third Class status, and sent to the Tasman Peninsula - *'to work in probationary gangs without wages and deprived of their liberty'*.

Political Prisoners

A new type of convict had now arrived at Port Arthur. They were classed as 'influential political prisoners'. The first prominent group were the Welsh Chartists, convicted of treason after the failed Newport Rising in Monmouthshire, England in 1839. Since their arrival in Van Diemen's Land, several of their ring-leaders had attempted to escape and were now assigned to incarceration at Port Arthur. Their names were John Frost, and Zephamiah Williams.

The causes the Welsh Chartists stood for and for which they were transported (causing unrest in the Queen's Realm in Great Britain), would not be considered at all unreasonable by today's standards. They stood for *the abolition of the 16 hour day*, abolition of child labour, and male suffrage (the right to vote).

Frost was a draper by profession and formerly the Mayor of Newport. Shortly after arrival he soon found himself in employment in the Commandant's office. Being an educated man his literacy skills were greatly appreciated. For then, as now, the *'paper-war'* with Head Offices has to go on! Zephamiah on the other hand, was a qualified mineral surveyor, and his skills were readily appreciated at the Saltwater River Coal Mines. It was not long after arrival that he was promoted to Superintendent of Mines even though he was a convict under sentence! Never could it be said that the prison staff at Port Arthur at that time were not pragmatists!

- Zephamiah Williams, Welsh Chartist -

Acting Comptroller General

In 1845, much building work was undertaken at the various convict outstations, and records reveal on the 30th June there were some 1,209 convicts located at Port Arthur itself. The Comptroller General Matthew Forster seemed well pleased, if his correspondence is to serve as a guide, as to the general state of affairs that year at the Port Arthur prison.

However in January 1846 the Comptroller died, and the Colonial Secretary recommended to the Governor that William Champ serve in an acting capacity in that position in Hobart until such time as the new incumbent could be selected. This was approved, with Captain L.F. Jones of the 96th Regiment standing in for Champ at Port Arthur as Acting Commandant. As events transpired, Commandant Champ was absent from Port Arthur for the period 22nd January 1846 to October 1846, on other duties.

Proposal to Construct a Penitentiary

By the mid 1840s pressure was now on for more suitable long term accommodation for the convicts. Personnel returns for June 1846 showed some 1200 on strength. The proposal was put up in August of that year, to construct a penitentiary to hold 1,000 men, and while supported in correspondence to England by the Governor, never materialised.

NOTICE.

PRISONERS admitted into Pentonville Prison will have an opportunity of being taught a Trade, and of receiving sound Moral and Religious Instruction. They will be transported to a Penal Colony, in Classes, as follows:—

FIRST CLASS.

Prisoners who shall, when sent from this Prison, be reported by the Governor and Chaplain to have behaved well.

These, at the end of 18 months, will be sent to Van Diemen's Land, to receive a Ticket of Leave, on landing, which, until forfeited by bad conduct, will, in that Country, confer most of the advantages of freedom. In Van Diemen's Land, labor being in great demand, and wages being therefore high, the Prisoner's knowledge of a trade, and the possession of a Ticket of Leave, will enable him, with industry and continued good conduct, to secure a comfortable and respectable position in Society. Prisoners who obtain Tickets of Leave may also, by industry and good conduct, acquire, in a short time, means sufficient to enable their families to follow them.

SECOND CLASS.

Prisoners who have not behaved well.

These, also, at the end of 18 months, will be transported to Van Diemen's Land where they will receive a Probationary Pass, which will secure to them only a limited portion of their earnings, will admit of their enjoying only a small portion of liberty, and will subject them to many restraints and privations.

THIRD CLASS.

Prisoners who have behaved ill.

These will be transported to Tasman's Peninsula, a Penal Colony, occupied only by Convicts and the Military Guard, there to be employed on the Public Works, in Probationary Gangs, without wages, and deprived of liberty; and their families will not be permitted, under any circumstances, to follow them.

Prisoners will see how much depends on their own conduct during their confinement in this Prison. According to their behaviour and improvement here, will be their future condition in the Colony to which they will be sent.

Stop-Start on Transportation
Early in 1846 the British Secretary of State for the Colonies, William Gladstone, had placed a temporary embargo for a period of two years on the transportation of convicts to V.D.L. The reason given, being to assist the colony in assimilating the large number of convicts that had previously arrived there. Confusion in the communication of this decision led some colonists to interpret the embargo to be of a finite nature, and when in 1848 further convicts arrived, it caused a civic furore which is further expanded in the next chapter.

The cessation in the flow of new convict arrivals in 1846, and then the uncertainty as to any future arrivals, made forward planning by the convict department, and particularly at Port Arthur, extremely difficult.

William Champ's Achievements
The main achievement secured by William Champ during his tenure were extensions to the Commandant's house, the fountain, the general layout of the Government Gardens, the construction of 'Officers Row', together with an avenue of white poplars which would lead to the infamous Model Prison, and whose construction was commenced in his last year as Commandant at Port Arthur.

- a stylised view of what the main Port Arthur gardens had become by the late 1840s -'

As history was to later dictate, William Champ's main claim to fame in Tasmanian political terms, lie elsewhere. He subsequently became the first Premier of Tasmania, when he stood in the first freely held elections, in 1856.

CHAPTER FIVE

A Period of Irreversible Change 1848-53

Transportation system under Review

In 1847 the decision was made by the British Government to close down the Norfolk Island Penal Station and transfer the convicts to Tasmania, with the *incorrigibles* to be incarcerated at Port Arthur. A general review was also being undertaken of the cost and effectiveness of the convict outstations on the Tasman Peninsula.

The new Comptroller of Prisons John Hampton put the proposal that:

" To make Port Arthur a place for severe and dreaded secondary punishment, I further submit for your Excellency's approval that, in connection with the above mentioned fifty Separate Apartments on the Pentonville Plan, a Penitentiary should be built."

John Hampton also took the initiative as to the general review of the convict stations and in his report to the Governor recommended that effective from the 30th June 1848, the position of Commandant be temporarily dispensed with as a cost saving measure, and that Superintendent G.H. Courtney be placed in charge of the day to day affairs at Port Arthur.

Superintendent G.H. Courtney - The Old Days No More

Superintendent Courtney set about his task of a detailed review of operations at Port Arthur with energy and perseverance. The drying up of the earlier supply of young convicts from Britain during the years 1846/47, had its toll on the convict outstations. Short of labour in comparison to the past, maintenance was needed on many projects and resolution of the Point Puer problem required action, even though now the number of boys had dropped significantly. Added to this, the general Port Arthur Regulations now required a major overhaul. At that time they were so drafted that only the Commandant had clear authority to make finite decisions, and such a person was now absent from the settlement!

*- part of the cast for the 1927 film based on Marcus Clarke's **For the Term of His Natural Life** film dressed in the appropriate period uniforms of that era in Champ street -*
(COURTESY PORT ARTHUR COLLECTION)

One of the first proposals from Superintendent Courtney (apart from his low opinion of the military officers there, in correspondence to the Comptroller he was to remark -*'the more officers are moved from here the better'*), was that the flour mill and granary, which had fallen into disuse, be converted to a Penitentiary. This proposal was not acted on in his time, and was left to his successor to implement.

The Port Arthur Settlement was now to undergo a series of changes that would irreversibly change its nature and purpose from being initially a 'happening and doing' place, which substantially assisted the colony's economy and development, to that of a 'social welfare' orientated institution which would prove to be a financial burden on both the British and Colonial Governments.

Its entrepreneurial dynamism, so clearly prominent in its early years when under the control of military Captains was now to be snuffed out, such that the activities base which James Boyd inherited as the new Commandant of Port Arthur on the 1st November 1853, would be a mere *shadow* of its former self.

No Longer a Captain of Industry
Let us now view in turn the combination of factors which led to the decline of Port Arthur as a major industrial base for the fledgling colony.

1. *The Commercial Pressures of Hobart Town:* The late 1840s, early 1850s were a very dynamic period in V.D.L's commercial history. Manufacturing, and the whaling industry were generating wealth for the more commercially gifted members of the colony, and this influential group felt restricted by the industrial base that had been built up at Port Arthur using 'government employed' convicts. They now cast their avaricious focus on the industries so well established at Port Arthur.

The first industry to be stripped from the Tasman Peninsula was boat-building and maritime repairs. The slips and yards were closed down on the grounds of alleged inefficiency in late 1848, early 1849. The next to go in the same year was the leasing out of the coal mines formerly controlled by the Port Arthur settlement, to private enterprise. The mines were handed over under the new lease on the 31st July 1848. The mines had lost apparently 3,000 pounds in 1847, and the expected annual savings in officers salaries alone was expected to be of the order of 2,000 pounds. Only the timber activities continued on, but at a slower pace. The accent was now on one of self-sufficiency as against export for use elsewhere in the colony.

2. *Closing down Point Puer - 1849:* At a domestic level, due to the negative report submitted by Benjamin Horne some six years earlier (1), a decision had at last been made by the authorities in 1849 to abandon Point Puer and relocate the boys to other facilities. Initially the intention was to re-house them at Safety Cove, but this was not proceeded with and those remaining were despatched to the convict station at Koonya, to Cygnet and Hobart Town.

In fact the winding down of Point Puer had commenced some three years earlier in England, with most of the young boys previously destined for transportation now remaining there to undergo Pentonvillian style correction at Parkhurst on the Isle of Wight, Great Britain.

3. *Closing down of Tramway and Semaphore Stations:* Both the tramway and semaphore chain of stations linking Port Arthur with Hobart had now been disbanded. The former because it was too expensive to maintain, the latter because cheaper forms of communication were now available.

4. *Effect of the Victorian Gold Rush -1851:* On another front, the discovery of gold in Victoria in 1851, initiated a mass exodus of ex convicts out of Van Diemen's Land to the mainland. Records reveal that in excess of 11,000 males under the age of 35, left the island in the first nine months of the discovery becoming public knowledge. In demographic terms this exodus while lifting the average age of those remaining (2) and removing the bite of an earlier labour glut, proved detrimental to the ongoing works programmes at Port Arthur. It shut off from the prison its normal incidental supply of future, young, 'second offenders'.

This local demise of 'fit young labour' to maintain the hard-labour work gangs on which the self sufficiency of the Prison depended, was further compounded by few recent arrivals being sent to the colony from overseas in the convict ships.

- Celebration marking the Cessation of Transportation Launceston V.D.L. 10 August 1853 -

5. *A Very Special Proclamation - August 1853:* The gates of circumstance finally shut their doors on Port Arthur (with respect to any future supply of young able-bodied men under sentence), on the 10th of August 1853. On that day the transportation of convicts to the Colony of Van Diemen's Land from England, was abolished.

It was the successful culmination of years of lobbying by the Launceston based *Anti-Transportation League.* Irreversible moods of change for independence from the mother country had become prominent in the late 1840s and early 1850s. Local citizens were now objecting violently to what previously had been accepted practice: that their colony serve as *the dumping ground* for the convicted felons of the English court system.

The British Government was in essence receptive to such concerns raised by the *'colonials'*, since it now appeared repugnant to the social reformers in London that, with the Victorian gold-rush in full spate, newly freed convicts might subsequently *profit* from their initial free transport (courtesy of the British government) to the Antipodes.

More Political Prisoners - William Smith O'Brien
One colourful dynamic that did occur during this period, was the arrival of a new set of political prisoners to V.D.L. They were the ring-leaders of the *Free Young Irish Movement,* who were colloquially referred to as the 'Seven Eagles'. Their outspoken 'clan chief' was the persuasive William Smith O'Brien, an Anglo-Irishman of aristocratic birth, and a member of the British House of Commons!

Of these only O'Brien spent time at the Port Arthur prison. This was because he consistently advised the authorities that he intended to escape from official confinement. Initially he had been placed on Maria Island, which had been specifically re-opened as a place of detention for him, but from where he had attempted to escape. With the status of now being a second offender (and having pointedly refused Lieutenant-Governor William Denison's request not to escape again), the authorities had no option but to place him under house arrest at Port Arthur!

- William Smith O'Brien -

- Maria Island settlement, considered too costly to relocate the Point Puer boys there, and from where William Smith O'Brien of the Free Young Irish Movement escaped such that he became a second offender and reposted to Port Arthur for a while -
(COURTESY PORT ARTHUR COLLECTION)

The authorities allocated O'Brien a converted stable for use as his living quarters. This building remains and can be inspected in the course of your visit. In an age of patronage his aristocratic status ensured that not only did he have a house of his own, but also he was assigned an overseer and an attendant to wash up his plates after each meal!

O'Brien's stay at Port Arthur was comparatively short-lived (5 months) for he eventually accepted his Ticket -of- leave, and like Frost before him, in later life, concentrated more on spirituality than politics.

- O'Brien's Cottage -

Alexander Cripps: One that Got Away - for a While!

While generally Port Arthur proved to be an efficient prison in terms of effectively retaining its inmates (or at least re-capturing them after a short period), there was the odd exception, and Alexander Cripps was one of these.

Cripps, a dog handler at Eaglehawk Neck, was sentenced to 14 months at Port Arthur for stealing dog food in the early 1850s. He escaped, went bush, and navigated his way back to Eaglehawk Neck where he stole two dogs. He then proceeded to live the life of a hermit with his dogs and it was only pure bad luck (or 'chance' -depending on how one views it) that 20 months later, he was caught.

What happened was that the Commanding Sergeant at the 'Neck' as part of his normal sporting recreational activities had, one Sunday afternoon, gone hunting wallaby. On entering a clearing he observed a dog on a leash tied to a tree with a leather muzzle over its mouth. On closer inspection he noticed it was one of his own dogs which had been stolen months earlier. A trap was set, and Cripps was followed back to his hideout, a substantial hut in a ravine in the middle of the wilderness.

Cripps had certainly been active with his time during his *unofficial leave of absence*, for located in the environs of the hut were no less than 150 dozen tanned wallaby skins! Given the entrenched philosophy of the times that absconders should not be seen to 'profit' from their daring escapes, these skins were later sold by Imperial Auction! It was also clear from the chattels located in the hut that Alexander Cripps during his 20 month respite in the Tasmanian bush, had made forays to the settlements to obtain supplies, from time to time.

Construction of the New Model Prison - 1849-53
Approval for the construction of the New Model Prison was received from England in early 1848. Work commenced in the first half of that year, and the first prisoners moved into the partly completed wing in 1849. Construction was completed in 1853.

The remains of this *'prison within a prison'*, and the bizarre psychological experiment it represented now serve as one of the main interpretation centres for the historic site. The bizarre procedures employed there, and the conditions imposed on the inmates, are covered in the next chapter.

Footnotes:
1. Horne's Report was very negative in its style and content: i.e. that there were problems with the soil, it was too windy and exposed to the elements, no water, very crowded and the general operational procedures for handling the juveniles -to his way of thinking- not strict enough.

2. Readers need to appreciate that this sudden departure of 11,000 young men did have a major impact on the fledgling colony, in the sense that it constituted *some 20% of the total European population* then living on the island.

- a photograph of the Model Prison shortly after closure -
(COURTESY PORT ARTHUR COLLECTION)

CHAPTER SIX

A Period of Shame 1853-56

- Government Cottage built 1853-54 for use by important visitors to Port Arthur -
(COURTESY PORT ARTHUR COLLECTION)

The Lessons of History

It is regrettable that in our busy lives and the minutiae of daily family pressures we do not take time to read more and reflect on the lessons of history, since human nature has changed very little over the centuries.

We now come to one of the most controversial periods in the history of the Port Arthur Settlement. On the one hand the new incoming Commandant James Boyd is regarded as one of the finest Prison Administrators the convict department ever recruited. He seemed to have advanced specialist views for the age, and from his writings appeared genuine in his desire to improve the welfare of the prisoners. Yet, despite all his sensibilities and attention to detail, Boyd did appear to have one major blind spot. He seemed unable to appreciate and was prepared to ignore the considered advice of his Medical Officers and others, as to the implicit treatment evils of the Separate Prison.

We are referring here to the *Model Prison* system of treatment for hardened criminals, which in the mirror prison at Pentonville in England was closed down in the 1850s, on the grounds that it *created more mental problems for the victim, than it ever cured.*

- James Boyd -
(COURTESY TAS FILM CORPORATION)

The above sketch of the 'B' Wing of the Separate Prison by an Unknown Artist (COURTESY
TASMANIAN FILM CORPORATION), is contemporary of the period. There was matting on the floor to
deaden sound by the patrolling warders. There were three cell wings in the Separate Prison,
two with 16 cells and 'B', with 18: nine down each side of the corridor as depicted in the above
sketch. The cells were small, 2 metres by 3 metres by 2.5 metres high. Inside each was a set of
corner shelves, sanitary bucket, small table and stool. Iron rungs were located at either end of
the cell from which the hammock was strung. Bedding consisted of two blankets and a rug.

- entrance to the Separate Prison's Solitary Cell -

(COURTESY PORT ARTHUR COLLECTION)

A Case for Social Conscience

We believe Boyd's failure to conduct a similar review of the practices of the Separate Prison in Tasmania (once the failures of the system had been fully exposed by the *Clapham Set* in London), unnecessarily spawned a tragic harvest of *prison generated* lunatics. Further, such a failure to act (apart from the mental cruelty imposed on the hundreds of victims that were 'processed' by the Model Prison), in turn generated great governmental expense in the 1860s and 70s in catering for their resultant needs as lunatics.

Certainly Tasmania may have been the main dumping ground for the whole of Britain's most anti-social outcasts for several decades, and certainly the worst of the worst may have ended up at Port Arthur as the place of last resort, short of being hanged. However, such an apologist argument we believe does slide off the point, that by the mid 1850s there was adequate evidence to hand at Port Arthur that the weird and outdated Benthamite theories of rehabilitation, when applied in practice had gone disastrously wrong.

Quite obviously James Boyd had a lot to contend with at that time, and what he achieved was most creditable (refer following notes as to the conversion of Granary to Penitentiary). However it does not add up that a man of his capacity chose to ignore the warning signals clearly emerging in the mid 1850s (if not earlier) as to the disastrous social side effects of the Separate Prison treatment programme. It is for this reason that we have chosen to call this section of the Port Arthur Settlement's history, *A Period of Shame*.

In coming to grips with this issue, we have found it most interesting to note quite independently that the Tasmanian Governor of that period (Lieutenant Governor Sir William Denison) shared a similar view of concern. On the subject, he wrote as follows to Colonel Joshua Jebb, the Inspector of Prisons in Great Britain:

"I have frequent intercourse with the Chaplains here and better opportunity of judging of the merits of the men of whom they speak can hardly corroborate your views of the efficacy of the separate system in producing repentance and amendment. Most efficient it is in our 50 cells as a means of punishment. Most heartily do the men dread the infliction, most carefully do they abstain from anything which may induce a return to such a place of confinement but as for reformation, for a real change of heart and life alas it can be expected from very few of them whose habits of crime have been so ingrained upon them as to lead them to become candidates for such a plan of extra punishment." (1)

Ian Brand in his book entitled Penal Peninsula has suggested that in expressing such a view, the Governor 'lacked understanding of the *principles behind the separate system of prison discipline'* (2). To the contrary, we suggest the Governor was astute in his observations appearing to be one of the few at that time to have sufficient vision to appreciate and note the potential dangers of such psychological experiments. Indeed we believe the key to Boyd's inexplicable inaction, may relate to his own future career prospects within the prison service.

He was after all, the prison warder who at Pentonville in England in the early 1840's, drafted the original Model Rules for Separate Prisons, which he then republished with respect to the Tasmanian Prison (Refer following page). His career was essentially built around being a *'Separate Prison system for Incorrigibles'* specialist, and with the era of transportation now over, the only mainstream area left which would command ongoing employment at a high salary, was in that area.

We suggest if one looks closely at the problems which confronted the convict department at that time (and add to this the reality that James Boyd was appointed to the position of Commandant Port Arthur at *three times the salary* previously granted to Superintendant Courtney (3) - when previously the position had been placed on the redundancy list for reasons of economy), then the patronage game-play of that time becomes clear.

No doubt the major challenge facing the department in the late 1840s, as seen through the eyes of the Comptroller General of Convicts John Hampton (4), was dealing with the die-hards, whose anti-social behaviour was beyond normal correction. With the Separate Prison System then appearing the logical way to go, and with James Boyd, the former Principal Warder of Pentonville already in Hobart serving as Superintendant of the Hobart Gaol (and therefore able to ensure its smooth running), it seemed inevitable with the power of hindsight, that such a rehabilitation programme would, in all probability, become entrenched in the state's penal system.

We will now take a closer look at the actual workings of the Separate Prison system after considering another thread of inconsistency which existed between the social classes, at that time.

Apartheid between the Classes.

The apartheid in the application of the Principles of Justice in the eighteenth and nineteenth century between the social class barriers was quite unreal. On the one hand a convict could be exposed to strict disciplinary measures for the slightest breach of the draconian prison rules and regulations, yet it was quite another issue for the Commandant to use convict labour at low rates to garden his own private plot of potatoes for sale on the Hobart market, or have greenhouses constructed by ticket-of-leave men and not pay them, condone his senior patron having stone quarried for his own private residence (5) or arrange timber to be felled and made into floor-boards by convicts for his own penal establishment, and not the government's set priorities.

RULES

FOR

PRISONERS,

SEPARATE PRISON.

261.—The prisoners are cautioned against committing any of the undermentioned offences, for which they will be liable to punishment, viz. :—communicating, or attempting to communicate with each other, either by words or signs ; reading aloud ; singing, dancing, or making any other noise whatever, except such as may be unavoidable in the performance of their allotted work ; not rising when the first bell is rung ; not keeping their persons, cells, and the various articles provided for their use at all times clean and neatly arranged ; leaving their cells improperly dressed, or without their badges ; not keeping their clothing in proper repair ; not maintaining the proper interval from each other when proceeding to or from the Chapel or Exercise-yards ; not behaving with due respect and decorum during Divine Service ; stopping any of the ventilating apertures ; marking, defacing, or damaging in any way their books or utensils ; wearing their caps in their cells ; not remaining visible to the Officers on duty during Divine Service ; not treating the Officers of the Estab-lishment and all visitors with due respect ; addressing any Officer or Constable, except for some necessary purpose ; not immediately reporting any article in their possession being broken or damaged by accident or otherwise ; having any unauthorised article whatever in their possession ; using their copy-books or slates for any anauthorised purpose ; unrolling their bedding before the bell has been rung for that purpose ; not extinguishing their cell lights and retiring to rest at the appointed signal ; taking down the lamps without permission ; allowing their lights to burn above a moderate height.

262.—Any prisoner wishing to see the Governor, the Comptroller-General, the Civil Commandant, the Chaplain, Medical Officer or the Schoolmaster, will intimate his desire to the Officer on duty.

263.—Any complaint respecting the quantity of food must be made before the article is taken into the cell.

264.—Any other complaint is to be made to the Commandant, or the Officer in Charge.

265.—A Copy of these Rules to be suspended in each Cell.

(Extracts from Port Arthur Approved Regulations.)

Separate Prison

In view of such a social tragedy being practised on site during this period in the life of the prison, it is suggested your stay at Port Arthur will not be complete without attempting to savour what life was like in those days, when the infamous Separate Prison was in operation.

You can do this by momentarily confining yourself to the darkness of one of the inner punishment cells, staring at the pulpit from the confines of one of the closed booths in the Chapel, or viewing the exercise yard and letting your imagination run free as to the dampness and isolation experienced by those men as they were returned once more after such solitary exercise, to the sombre silence of their respective cells; while their warders warmed themselves close to the hearth fire at the end of the cell block!.

Model Prison in Operation

The Pentonvillian style Model Prison and the social experiment it symbolised, was largely imposed on the older generation of incorrigible convicts either transferred from Norfolk Island or from the pool of die-hards already located in the main penitentiary.

As a direct result of the treatments practiced in the Model Prison, the incidents of mental disability amongst its inmates by the late 1850s, had now begun to climb to an alarming level.

From all accounts it appears as though the local authorities under James Boyd at Port Arthur were not prepared to deal in a concerned manner with the psychological traumas they were now generating, amongst the inmates of the Separate Prison. They simply noted for the record the outcome, classing the casualties as being permanently deranged (lunatics); that if released at some future time, they would never again play a useful role in society.

With the hindsight of history, we can at the very least observe it was indeed tragic that there was no such equivalent to the 'Clapham Set' in the colonies to serve as a mentor for ongoing prison practices at Port Arthur, during Boyd's period as Commandant.

Why did the Theory Fail?

Bearing all this in mind, it is instructional for the reader to take a closer look at this system of life imposed on the inmates of the Model Prison at Port Arthur, and consider why it promoted mental derangement amongst its clients.

- Reverend Eastman (1859-1870) in the church pulpit in the Separate Prison Chapel. He was not a popular man and appeared unsympathetic to the genuine welfare needs of the convicts -
(COURTESY TASMANIAN MUSEUM AND ART GALLERY)

- Watch clock in the Separate Prison. Duty Warder would be fined for every peg not pushed in exactly every quarter of an hour during the course of the night. A symbol of the relentlessness of the Penopticon model for cold efficiency and attention to the smallest of details. -

(COURTESY QUEEN VICTORIA MUSEUM AND ART GALLERY)-

The 'nature of the beast' appears to have been that the **Penopticon** system of prison reform, was innately flawed from the outset. It inexplicably combined into a single prisoner rehabilitation programme, conflicting principles of dealing both humanely and inhumanely with fellow human beings, completely under one's control.

On the one hand prisoners were to be regularly exercised, attend church, and adequately occupied with an 'honest days work'. In their confined cells, they were fed an adequate diet, and physical abuse abolished (e.g. no more flogging). Yet, on the other side of the coin major *abuses of the mind* were practised. In particular the basic human desire *to communicate with one's fellow beings* was specifically denied. Extraordinary lengths were taken to secure anaesthetised isolation of the individual.

Matting was on the floor, not for comfort or warmth under foot, but to block out the sound of one's tread. Exercising hoods were worn over the head, during the exercise periods, so that one was denied even glancing at one's fellow inmate. At church, silence had to be strictly observed (never did a preacher have such a captive audience!), and the pews were specifically designed (as you can see for yourselves), to maintain isolation even though one was part of the congregation.

In the punishment cells, the unrelenting darkness ensured that you could not see the hand in front of your face, and your diet was bread and water. You might be incarcerated in such a fashion for a few days, or in some instances up to thirty days!

The Model Prison at Port Arthur therefore serves as a tangible reminder in stark terms, as to the power and devastation an unsound theoretical idea can have on society if translated into practice, then allowed to continue unchecked and unquestioned.

Conversion of Granary to Penitentiary

One of the first major building tasks which confronted Boyd on taking up the position of Commandant in 1853 was to carry through the initial recommendation of Superintendent Courtney some years previous, to convert the granary and treadmill complex, into a new Penitentiary.

In a report relating to the reconstruction, it was stated that the building was 230 feet long, four stories high and 38 1/2 feet wide. Two stories of cells contained in the lower part were arranged in double rows end to end, with their fronts facing the external walls of the prison. Work commenced on the project on the 1st of September 1854, the land in front of it was reclaimed in 1855 and the pile wharf was constructed in 1856.

The Penitentiary was finally completed on the 22nd April 1857, and consisted of 136 separate cells on the lower floors for prisoners under heavy sentence. Above the cells was a spacious dining room approximately 160 feet long, 32 feet wide and 12 feet high. This open space also doubled as a school room, assembly place for Roman Catholics and had a library room annexed. The upper floor was a general dormitory area 200 feet long and 11 feet high designed to accommodate 348 separate sleeping places in two tiers. At the back were the exercise yards, privies and lavatories.

- a view of the Dormitories on the top floor of the Penitentiary -
(COURTESY TASMANIAN MUSEUM AND ART GALLERY)

- a view of the Entrance Hall of the Penitentiary -
(COURTESY TASMANIAN MUSEUM AND ART GALLERY)

- a photograph taken shortly after closure providing us with a good view of the inside of the penitentiary from the main foyer, showing the location of the cell blocks and the stairways leading to the dining room on the second floor and the dormitories above. -
(COURTESY ARCHIVES OFFICE OF TASMANIA)

- a closer view of the ground floor in the cell gallery. In contrast to the much later photograph taken (and published on the next page) it can be seen that cleanliness and neatness was very much part of prison discipline. A bell system was a feature of these cells with inmates being able to summon a gaoler through the device of a bell lever in their cell sounding an alarm and their cell number plate swinging out from the outside wall. -
(COURTESY ARCHIVES OFFICE OF TASMANIA)

- This graphic photograph taken many years after closure (and therefore portraying a state of neglect and dirt which would not have been tolerated during the life of the prison) does however provide us with a clear insight into the 'sharp end' of convictism. It is a close up photograph of the entrance to one of the solitary cells on the lower floor of the Penitentiary, as generally shown in the bottom photograph on page 51. In Imperial measurements these cell boxes were approximately 4 feet wide, 10 feet long and 8 feet high. Complete with peephole and small trapdoor in the door to pass in food, conditions inside the cells were extremely spartan for the inmates. The hammock was slung from ironwork embedded in the wall, a small hole (clearly seen in the photograph) served as a crude form of ventilation, and three simple plank-type corner shelves performed regimented functions. On the top shelf was placed the rolled hammock, the middle held the water cask or pitcher, and the bottom shelf plates and eating utensils.

(COURTESY TASMANIAN FILM CORPORATION)

Other Activities

1856 also saw the extension of timber and felling operations to supply timber for the new Government House in Hobart Town.

Footnotes

1. Jebb Papers Box No 4 Undated
2. page 106
3. Boyd's salary per annum was set at £600, while Courtney's had been £200
4. Hampton and Boyd had travelled out together to Australia on the same convict ship, the *Sir James Seymour* in 1844 and had renewed their friendship when Boyd became Superintendent of the Prisoners Barracks Hobart in the late 1840s.

5. The Comptroller General was involved in a major scandal involving him receiving for his own private residence at Boa Vista stone quarried by convicts and Boyd as Commandant was implicated in allowing the convicts to do the work for his patron. Questions were raised in the Legislative Council as a result of the matter commanding newspaper headlines and editorials in the *Tasmanian Daily News*. Hampton refused to appear before a Select Committee of Councillors and was ultimately forced to leave the colony as a result of the impasse to avoid arrest, and then made a career elsewhere in Western Australia.

- a view from the steps of the Commandant's residence down Champ street -
(COURTESY ARCHIVES OFFICE OF TASMANIA)

CHAPTER SEVEN

End of an Era 1856 - 77

Elections and a Name Change

The year 1856 was to serve as a milestone in the history of Tasmania. Not only was it the year that the state changed its name from Van Diemen's Land to Tasmania, but also for the first time *free elections* were held on a limited franchise basis. *'Limited franchise'* meant that only the comparatively wealthy (which were only a small proportion of the total population) were eligible to vote. Even so, it was a great leap forward in terms of the constitutional maturing of the colony. The former Commandant of Port Arthur, William Thomas Napier Champ, became the first freely elected Premier of Tasmania. This in part underscores the important role Port Arthur had played in the past in the development of the fledgling colony.

No Longer in the Centre of Events

However, as indicated in the last chapter, Port Arthur in the late 1850s was a very different place from what it had been merely a decade earlier. With no young men left, it had been relegated essentially to that of an *institution* for a disadvantaged ageing group of exiled males. These men bore the scars of the transportation system, and the wounds they had incurred were both visible (physical), and invisible (mental).

At a time when kith and kin and the extended family was the norm, these broken men were now *cultural solitary exiles*. No longer young, the heritage of a different era, these remaining Port Arthur inmates felt mentally estranged from the world, which now seemed to be passing them by outside the bounds of their open prison surrounds. The nature of their entrenched plight promoted the responsible government of the day in Tasmania to acknowledge their difficulties, and belatedly remedial measures of sorts were put in place to mitigate the social tragedy.

Construction of the Paupers Mess

The outcome (given that the British Government did not wish to see these broken and deranged individuals repatriated back to Great Britain) was the construction of what was termed the *'Paupers Mess'*. In neutral functional terms it was in essence an *'old man's home'*. In 1864 records show that there were 167 ex convicts housed at the Paupers Mess, and 111 of those individuals were considered by the authorities to be mentally insane.

- The Paupers or Invalid's Mess Hall is seen here in the left foreground with the later built Asylum in the centre to rear of the photograph, which was taken sometime after closure but before the devastating 1895 bushfires -
(COURTESY TASMANIAN MUSEUM AND ART GALLERY)

Off to the Maori Wars - 1864
Also it was in this year, that the British soldiery left destined never to return, having departed to New Zealand to take part in the Maori wars.

There was now only one Regiment left in Tasmania, and that was stationed at Hobart Town. The rest had literally left over-night. All had relinquished their normal colonial guarding duties within twenty four hours of the Movement Orders being received. Their sudden departure left matters in a state of chaos. Particularly at Port Arthur, where only recently the Paupers Mess had been brought into operation caring for a large number of mentally unstable individuals.

This quandary prompted a new initiative at the local level. The less physically active convicts in the general barracks area were now given the task of caring for the paupers, and at times visitors and observers could be forgiven for asking the salient question as to *who* was leading *whom?*

Construction of the Lunatic Asylum
The last major building activity to be put in place at Port Arthur during this period, was the Lunatic Asylum. It was built in 1867. Due to the age of the men on site now, the authorities were forced to employ *free mechanics* (term used in those days for building tradesmen) to assist in the building's completion. The costs of its construction was born by the British Government: to serve as some measure of compensation for the reality that these men would never be allowed to return to their native shore.

- photograph of the Asylum circa 1896 when serving as Carnavon Town Hall -
(COURTESY PORT ARTHUR COLLECTION)

Departure of James Boyd
On the 31st May 1871 James Boyd stepped down as Commandant. While Boyd undoubtedly served for the longest period as Commandant (1853-71), and he came to the position as allegedly the first professional Prison Administrator, we consider his efficiency in terms of taking reasonable care of the prisoners placed under his almost total control, should be seriously questioned. He appeared to be (in direct contrast to the the military predecessors before him who were able to utilize the convict workforce in imaginative ways to assist the young colony), to be that of being strictly a Prison Warder. Boyd appeared shackled to the philosophy of the penopticon mode of rehabilitation of hardened offenders, despite clear warnings that it created more mental disabilities than it cured, and we believe many convicts suffered unduly because of this. His successor, a Mr Adolarius Boyd (not a relative) took up duties as the new Commandant on the 1st June 1871, and was to remain at the post until the 31st March 1874.

Autumn of an Era

Within this decade the majority of the remaining men at Port Arthur, who had first arrived as fit young convicts, were in the winter of their lives. Many were beyond their 80th year. As the prison was now no longer a self-sufficient entity and was proving to be a financial drain on state coffers, and no credible justification could be raised in argument for its continuance, the decision was finally made to close down the institution for good.

Turning Full Circle

Significant moments in social history are often heralded in real life not by a fanfare or a ceremony, but by a simple everyday act. At Port Arthur it was simply one of the departure of a brig called the **Harriet** on the 17th September 1877, just under two weeks short of the 47th Anniversary of the first convicts landing there in 1830. On that September day in 1877, the last remaining contingent of 7 convicts boarded the brig in transit to their new home which was to be the Campbell Street Gaol, Hobart Town.(1)

The dictates of circumstance had turned full circle for Port Arthur. Just as the first Commandant had been both Doctor and Commandant so too had the last (Dr John Coverdale 1st April 1874 -17th September 1877), and indeed the number of convicts that departed on the last day had been less than those who had originally arrived there in the spring of 1830.

- empty mess hall on the floor of the Penitentiary building devoid of furniture, shortly after closure. One can imagine how a singular visitor would find the silence deafening and the tread of their feet on the wooden boards unnaturally loud as they walked the length of the room and then returned to shut the door on their departure.. -
(COURTESY TASMANIAN MUSEUM AND ART GALLERY)

The Last Day 17th September 1877
One can imagine as these last seven inmates of Port Arthur boarded the *Harriet* and perhaps glanced back quickly to take in a last fleeting look of the settlement, that the impression was one of unnerving stillness. The Complex of buildings of a bygone era (inside whose stout walls, many of the rooms with their fittings left untouched (2) had a psychic clamouring of misery, sweat and tears), now stood desolate and unpeopled. A landscape of English trees, ornate shrubbery and rose gardens, left to the preserve of the chatter of blackbirds. It was an historic oddity located in a remote area and somewhat out of place in the midst of an Australian coastline of burnt hues, eucalypt, cliffs, rocks, ocean swell and foam.

The final chapter in the British-initiated Transportation saga, had now well and truly drawn to a close.

Cleansing By Fire
The memories and cultural structures at the Port Arthur Historic Site, which had so irreversibly effected the lives of so many individuals, was only really cleansed by the ritual of fire in 1895, when the first of two severe bushfires (the other in 1897), effectively reduced the site to the ruins that you see today. The ongoing history of Port Arthur from that time to the present and the restoration programmes that have since been put in place, are outside the bounds of this history.

However, it suffices for you, the Reader, to know that the social stigma of the name Port Arthur at the time of closure in 1877 was such that the locality was re-named *Carnavon* in 1878. It was not until 1932, with the passage of time healing the wounds, and a certain change in attitude (with even the sons of convicts fighting alongside the former gaolers of their parents in the First World War), that the site was re-named once more, Port Arthur.

Let it be said therefore, that your visit to Port Arthur Historic Site has been not only an enjoyable, interesting and memorable experience, but also just a little disquieting - *there but for the Grace of God go I ?*

Alex Graeme-Evans
Michael Ross
December 1992

Footnotes:

1. Dr Coverdale reported as having under his care on the 1st January 1877 64 (in other correspondence the number is stated as 83) prisoners, 126 paupers and 79 lunatics. On the 17th April 1877, all paupers and lunatics, and 47 prisoners left Port Arthur on the *Southern Cross*. While it is unclear how and when the other 10 (or 29 if the earlier figure of 83 is accepted as accurate) prisoners departed the site, it is clear there were only seven left to embark on the *Harriet* on the 17th September.

2. Fittings in the Penitentiary, Paupers Mess, Hospital, Asylum, and Separate Prison had been left untouched. Only movable furniture and the clocks from both the Church and the Penitentiary had been removed and transported to Hobart. All livestock, the schooner *Harriet*, and three other boats were disposed of by public auction. The facilities and grounds were now opened up for free settlement.

- prior to the devastating mid 1890s bushfires which rampaged through the settlement Port Arthur, under its new name Carnavon, was re-peopled once more. This time, by holiday makers in an era when staying at boarding houses was popular. This particular boarding house Trenville, had developed out of official's quarters, but was lost in the 1897 bushfire. Of historic interest in the foreground is not only one of the original mini-semaphores used to communicate within the confines of the settlement before the introduction of the telephone, but also beside it is reputed to be devoid of its bogies, the remains of the VIP carriage used on the wooden railway line which ran from Norfolk Bay (Taranna) to Long Bay (Oakwood) -
(COURTESY ARCHIVES OFFICE OF TASMANIA)

- due to its location, stature and positioning within the settlement, the Commandant's residence became the popular Carnavon Hotel, and was one of the few major structures to avoid the ravages of the mid 1890s bushfires -
(COURTESY ARCHIVES OFFICE OF TASMANIA)

Exercise Yard
Separate Prison

This was one of the original twelve exercise yards which formed part of the Model Prison complex.

Prisoners were allowed to exercise for one hour a day each day, but only on their own.

This yard had a metal grid over it because one enterprising inmate, a former chimney sweep, was able to escape its confines by grabbing hold of the bars on the window seen in the top right (which provided light to the Chapel) and from there scrambling over the wall.

Each yard was triangular in shape, and contained a small shelter so that prisoners might continue to exercise on wet days.

(COURTESY ARCHIVES OFFICE OF TASMANIA)

Further Reading

While by no means comprehensive the following may assist in providing you with further insights into this fascinating era in Australia's history. Fictional : 'The Men who God forgot' R. Butler; 'For the Term of his Natural Life' Marcus Clarke; 'Escape to Eagle hawk' V. Farrer. General : 'Convicts and Colonies' A.G.L. Shaw; 'Convict Worker' S. Nicholas; 'Fatal Shore' R. Hughes: 'Convict Australia 1788-1868' B. Vance Wilson ; 'Penal Peninsula' I. Brand; 'A Place of Misery' M. Weidenhofer; 'A History of Australia Vols 1-6' Manning Clark; 'A Short History of Australia' R. Ward; 'A History of Tasmania' L.L. Robson; 'Young Male Convicts in Van Diemens Land' K. Humfrey; 'Design for Convicts' J. Semple-Kerr; 'Criminal Prisons of London' H. Mayhew & J. Binney; 'Fate of the Artful Dodger' P. Buddee; 'Heart of Exile' P. Adam Smith; 'The Bligh Note Book' Editor J. Bach; 'Notorious Strumpets and Dangerous Girls' P. Tardiff.

INDEX

Aikenhead, James 33
Albury State Prison 31
Anti-Transportation League 33, 39
Arthur, Gov. George 3, 7, 12
Backhouse, James 18
Banks, Joseph 5
Bentham, Jeremy 5
Betsy Island 31
Birchs Bay 7
Booth, Capt. Charles O'Hara 15, 16, 21, 23, 26, 30, 31, 32, 33
Botany Bay 6
Bowen, Lt. John 6
Boyd, Adorlarius 55
Boyd, James 38, 42, 44, 45, 47, 49, 53, 55
Bushfires 31, 57, 58
Carnavon 57
Cascades 20
Cat-O-Nine-Tails 12
Centipede gangs 11
Champ, William Thomas Napier 33, 34, 36, 54
China 6
Clapham Set 44, 47
Clarke, Marcus 33, 37
Clothing 12
Coal Mines 20, 31
Collins, Lt. Gov. David 6, 7
Convictism 3
Cook, James 5
Courtney, Superintendent 37, 49
Coverdale, Dr. John 56, 58
Cripps, Alexander 40, 41
Cygnet 38
D'Entrecasteaux Channel 26
Declaration of Independence 4
Denison, Lt.-Gov. William 39, 44
Drake, Admiral 3
Eagle, Elizabeth Charlotte 23
Eaglehawk Neck 40
Eastman, Rev. 47
Eleanor 31
Elisa 31, 32
Emily Downing 31
Fanny 31
Forest, Anne 32
Forestier's Peninsula 32
Forster, Matthew 34
Frances Charlotte 17
Franklin, Lady Jane 24
Frederick 19, 31
Free election 54
Free Young Irish Movement 39
Frost, John 34
Fusiliers 15
Gibbons, Lt. John 10
Gladstone, William 36

Government House 19
Great Britain 2, 4, 34
Hampton, John 37, 45, 53
Harriet 56, 57, 58
Hippolyte Rocks 31
HMS Endeavour 5
Hobart 3, 6, 9, 15, 16, 19, 26, 31, 34, 38, 45, 53, 55, 56
Horne, Benjamin 17, 33, 38, 41
Hoy, David 19, 31
Hulks 4, 5
Impression Bay 20
Incorrigibles 7, 9, 10, 37, 45
Industrial Revolution 4
Invalid's Mess Hall 22
Isabella 31
Isle of the Dead 13
Jones, Capt. L.F. 34
King George III 5, 6
King Island 7
King James I 4
Koonya 38
Lady Franklin 18, 31
Lady Nelson 6
Lampriere Family 32
Lang, Henry 24, 31
Launceston Examiner 33
Legislative Council 53
Limited franchise 54
Long Bay 26, 58
Macquarie Harbour 8, 9, 19
Mahon, Capt. John 10
Mainwaring, Major F. 33
Manton, Rev. John A. 13
Maori Wars 55
Miller, Linus 23
Model Separate Prison 36, 41, 42-48
Molesworth Select Committee 23
Molesworth, Sir William 31
Newport Rising 34
Norfolk Bay 26, 58
Norfolk Island 31, 47
O'Brien, William Smith 39, 40
Officer's Row 36
Panopticon 33, 48
Parkhurst 38
Passenger tramway 26, 27
Pentonville 33, 34, 35, 37, 42, 45, 47
Phillip, Gov. Arthur 6
Point Puer 2, 10, 16, 17, 18, 20, 33, 37, 38
Popham, Sir Hugh 26
Port Jackson 6
Prison farms 7
Probationary System 23
Probationers 33
Queen Elizabeth I 3

Queen's Orphanage 32
Rebellion of Upper Canada 23
Risdon Cove 6
River Derwent 6
Russell, Capt. Assist-Surgeon John 8, 10
Saltwater River 20, 34
Second offenders 7
Semaphore system 26
Seymour, Sir James 53
Skilly 12
'Sloping Main' 20
Smith O'Brien's cottage 22, 40
Southern Cross 58
Spanish Armada 3
Sullivan's Cove 6
Swanston, Capt. 31
Sydney 6, 9, 26
Tamar 17
Tasman Peninsula 3
Tasman, Abel 6
Tasmanian Daily News 53
Terra nullus 6
The Chapel 46, 47
The Derwent 31
The First Fleet 6
The Granary 49
The Lunatic Asylum 55
The Paupers Mess 54, 58
Transportation Act 4
Transportation 3, 4, 33, 57
Victorian Gold Rush 38
Watch Clock 48
Watson, John 19
Webb, Col. Joshua 44
Wedge Bay 20
Welsh Chartists 34
West, Rev. John 33
Williams, Zephamiah 34